MIDCOURSE CORRECTION FOR THE
COLLEGE CLASSROOM

MIDCOURSE CORRECTION FOR THE COLLEGE CLASSROOM

Putting Small Group Instructional Diagnosis to Work

Carol A. Hurney, Christine M. Rener, and Jordan D. Troisi

Foreword by Mary Deane Sorcinelli

STERLING, VIRGINIA

Published by Stylus Publishing, LLC.
22883 Quicksilver Drive
Sterling, Virginia 20166-2019

Library of Congress Cataloging-in-Publication-Data
CIP data for this title is forthcoming.

13-digit ISBN: 978-1-64267-312-8 (cloth)
13-digit ISBN: 978-1-64267-313-5 (paperback)
13-digit ISBN: 978-1-64267-314-2 (library networkable e-edition)
13-digit ISBN: 978-1-64267-315-9 (consumer e-edition)

Printed in the United States of America

All first editions printed on acid free paper
that meets the American National Standards Institute
Z39-48 Standard.

Bulk Purchases

Quantity discounts are available for use in workshops and
for staff development.

Call 1-800-232-0223

First Edition, 2022

To all of the courageous and inspirational teachers who welcomed us into their classrooms

CONTENTS

I am delighted to write this foreword, not only because Carol A. Hurney, Christine M. Rener, and Jordan D. Troisi have been Professional and Organizational Development (POD) Network colleagues for many years, but also because I believe deeply in the value of the small group instructional diagnosis (SGID) for all instructors. I also believe that educational developers at every stage of their careers can enrich and strengthen their professional practice by learning about the research and practice on SGID presented in this book. At its core, the SGID provides an instructor with student feedback on a course while the course is in progress. Its outcomes are timely, targeted, and actionable instructional improvements that can help teachers and educational developers alike enhance the quality of student learning.

My own introduction to individual consultation came during my graduate internship in the Clinic to Improve University Teaching, University of Massachusetts Amherst (UMass). I was trained in the teaching improvement process, a four-stage sequence of data collection, data analysis, improvement strategies, and assessment. I carried this model, which included an initial interview, class observation, videotaping, and student questionnaire, to Indiana University Bloomington where I led a faculty development program. A decade later, I founded a center for teaching and learning (CTL) at UMass. By then, however, I knew that I needed to find a consultation model that was comprehensive, yet more streamlined, student-centered, and instructor-friendly. I found that model in the SGID.

When Carol Hurney proposed the idea of a comprehensive book on the SGID, I was thrilled. The SGID has been a cornerstone program in our CTL (we call it the "Midterm Assessment Program") since the early 1990s. Over the decades I've seen the extent to which instructors have gained insights into their teaching, as well as identifying specific strategies to improve their instruction, and how students have learned in their classes. Students have benefited in other ways from participating in an SGID: They have been given opportunities to examine their assumptions about teaching and reflect on their learning. Instructors reported that the experience helped to open a dialogue with their students on teaching and learning, increased the level of trust between student and teacher, and contributed to an effective learning environment.

For years, Hurney, Rener, and Troisi have been developing and refining SGID programs on their own campuses, exploring the practice of SGID and studying its impact on teaching knowledge and behaviors as well as on student learning. At the annual POD Network conference, I listened with interest and enthusiasm as Carol Hurney described how the SGID had become a signature service of her (and her coauthors') CTLs and how powerful and transformative the process can be as a source for substantive, meaningful student feedback and pedagogical improvement.

The most recent large-scale study of the field of educational development in the United States and Canada (Beach et al., 2016) also found that educational developers and instructors highly value SGIDs for their confidential, relational, and focused support. For example, in phone interviews following our web-based survey to developers, we asked CTL directors to identify one signature approach—a program they believed was of the highest quality or was the most recognized on their campuses. One director spoke for others in choosing her CTL's SGID program as the one initiative the center would offer if only allowed a single program in its portfolio. Perhaps this is why the SGID was also identified by CTL directors as an approach that they would either add to their portfolios or expand if given the resources to do so, and this was especially true for developers in liberal arts and community colleges.

Yet despite the SGID's desired use by a growing number of CTLs, learning about it has been challenging, in part because SGIDs go by so many different names that it is hard to follow the breadcrumbs, both in scholarship and practice. This book, then, fills an important gap in the literature on the SGID, and offers a valuable guide to the intellectual and practical work of this compelling approach to consultation. The authors introduce the reader to the SGID with narratives about their early SGID encounters. They describe the tasks necessary for SGID consultants to design and implement the process, replete with infographics and checklists. They argue for flexibility in use, offering SGID variations that accommodate local needs, challenges, and circumstances. The authors present lessons learned for growing and enhancing an SGID program. They also describe the influence of SGID on instructors' courses as well as its promise for advancing the culture of teaching at departmental and campus levels. Finally, they examine ways to document its impact on students, faculty, and campus culture and suggest opportunities for future research on the SGID.

All told, the authors have delivered the first one-stop, comprehensive guide to SGID in a research-informed, direct, and exceptionally readable style. They break down the last few decades of scholarship and practice on the SGID into coherent, useful, and well-organized advice, keeping the needs and interests of instructors and educational developers front and center, to the benefit of student learning. The drawing together of existing research and examples from the authors' experiences in starting, renewing, and evaluating SGID programs will guide readers as they develop an SGID program and integrate it with other CTL services.

Hurney, Rener, and Troisi's *Midcourse Correction for the College Classroom* is a powerful tool for educational development practice and a must-read for faculty and educational developers striving for improvement. It can support the development of a shared vision and understanding of SGID and can flexibly be used with both individual faculty and colleague-based programs, across career stages and institutional types. Imagine a book that is like having a respected and trusted faculty colleague just down the hall, ready with a wonderful array of lessons learned and insights. That is this book.

—Mary Deane Sorcinelli
Coprincipal Investigator, Undergraduate STEM Education Initiative,
Association of American Universities (AAU)
Professor Emeritus and Founding Director, Center for Teaching
and Faculty Development, University of Massachusetts Amherst

ACKNOWLEDGMENTS

This book would have not been possible without the exceptional community of educational development colleagues within the POD Network in Higher Education. We have benefited greatly from opportunities to learn about many aspects of the field and the SGID itself. The annual conferences have provided a venue to share our SGID work and hear valuable feedback and insights during sessions and over meals. The POD Network afforded a particularly important occasion to survey members as part of our research for this book. The responses from over 200 educational developers and the subset of follow-up interviews were instrumental in informing our work and we extend a special note of gratitude for all who gave of their time, reflections, and insights. We are particularly indebted to Mary Deane Sorcinelli for providing a foreword for this book and for her unwavering support of our work.

Carol A. Hurney

I stand on the shoulders of many people who guided my career in educational development and worked with me to champion the SGID. I am endlessly thankful to Marva Barnett, who welcomed me into the Teaching Resource Center at the University of Virginia as a faculty consultant. Not only did I experience the SGID under Barnett's guidance, I learned about the field of educational development, which became my life's work and passion. I thank Kit Murphy and the rest of my GenEd biology colleagues at James Madison University for welcoming the student voice into our pedagogical design process through the SGID. There are not enough words to express my gratitude to Karen Santos, who supported me as we worked together to grow the Center for Faculty Innovation (CFI) and build a thriving SGID program. She believed in me and the magic of the SGID. I also thank the rest of my CFI colleagues, especially Ed Brantmeier, Andreas Broscheid, Douglas Harrison, Tanya Laffler, Dianne Little, Cara Meixner, and Tiffany Runion, for walking alongside me as we developed activity plans, reimagined the impact of our work, and built new bridges to support the work of the JMU faculty. I am especially thankful for the opportunity to work with an exceptional group of faculty fellows, especially Jennifer Almjeld, Taz Daughtry, Beth Eck, Jamie Frye, Steve Harper, Nancy Harris, Natalie Kerr, Susan Kruck, Patrice Ludwig, Smita Mathur, Carole Nash, Olga Pierrakos, and Sam Prins, who brought their passion for teaching and learning to our collective work. For the million ways I am a better teacher and educational developer, I applaud my students who revealed to me the things I could not see on my own. I admire my new colleagues and students at Colby College for embracing the SGID and working with me to create a thriving CTL. I am forever grateful to my coauthors for believing in this book and for their insights, wisdom, and laughter. Finally, I dance in the kitchen and sing all her favorite songs to thank my wife, Aura, who inspires me to be my gypsy.

Christine M. Rener

I owe an enormous debt of gratitude to the faculty, staff, and students at Grand Valley State University, whom I have had the pleasure to learn from and with over the past decade. Not a day goes by when I am not acutely aware of how much my educational development efforts are not only made possible but buoyed by the creative, energetic, and collaborative campus environment at this institution. I sincerely thank Maria C. Cimitile, former provost and executive vice president for academic and student affairs, for her unwavering support of my work and for her perceptive encouragement to pursue scholarly projects. Both as a colleague and an academic leader, I could ask for no better model of and champion for professional excellence and lifelong learning. My colleagues in the Robert and Mary Pew Faculty Teaching and Learning Center, without whom the SGID journey would not have been possible, deserve special words of appreciation: Barb Blankemeier, Patty Stow Bolea, David Eick, Kurt Ellenberger, Dana Munk, Thomas Pentecost, Raquel Ramirez, and Kathryn Stieler. You have each shaped our SGID program in so many ways and I am grateful to be part of such a fabulous team. My early educational development adventures would not have been possible without Gregory Baer, Daniel Miller, and Dennis Munk of Carthage College. Thank you for making it so much fun to build a center, design programs, write reports, and learn together. If the process of writing a book has taught me anything, it has been that collaboration matters. I am deeply grateful for the experience of working with my coauthors. The time we have spent—virtually and in person—has been a joy and I could not have wished for a better collaborative process. Finally, I want to thank my partner, Rob, for his unwavering support. The gifts of time, memes, and coffee have made all of the difference.

Jordan D. Troisi

I want to acknowledge the many individuals who first saw and drew out the potential in me as an educational developer. At Sewanee: The University of the South, these individuals include Deon Miles and Betsy Sandlin, who were the first, and some of the best, educational developers I have ever met. They believed in me enough to help me become the codirector of the Center for Teaching there. I also wish to thank some other stalwart colleagues in educational development at Sewanee, including Emily Puckette, who served as the codirector of the Center for Teaching with me with such grace and patience, as well as Kate Cammack and Rae Manacsa, who were insightful and reflective colleagues in all of their work with faculty. Kate Cammack was also the first individual to conduct an SGID in one of my own courses, and I am indebted to her for her skillfully delivered feedback and conversation about the SGID process. I also wish to express my thanks to two other individuals who have shepherded my development from an early age as leaders in the Society for the Teaching of Psychology. Andrew Christopher of Albion College was my mentor through my 4 undergraduate years, and his support of my personal and professional endeavors has been steadfast over the last 2 decades. If there is a better mentor of undergraduate students, I would be surprised. Additionally, I wish to thank Aaron Richmond of the Metropolitan State University of Denver for his wisdom and humor as I approached new professional leadership roles, including my service as the director of the Annual Conference on Teaching. Allow me to also thank my coauthors, who introduced me to the SGID process and made the challenge of writing a book on it feel more like a conversation around a coffee table, at least most of the time. Lastly, I wish to thank my wife, Lauren, for believing in me much more than I do. Her genuine support as I worked on portions of this book was inexhaustible.

INTRODUCTION

Setting the Stage

I'm not sure when I started to embrace student feedback about my teaching, but I do know that in my first teaching position, I was disappointed that nobody— none of my biology colleagues, not my department chair, not even my mentor— came into my class to watch my teaching. Thus, the only feedback I had was from my students and that only came in large, often unpleasant doses, at the end of each semester. I felt like things were going well, but it is hard to say when you are teaching a large-enrollment, introductory biology course for nonmajors. I knew they were doing okay on the exams—not great, but okay. I also knew that most of them were coming to class and participating in the active learning exercises. However, sometimes I wasn't sure if I was really connecting with them. It seemed like I could simply ask them how things were going, but given the power dynamics of the college classroom, I knew that would be a foolish endeavor. So I swallowed my doses of end-of-semester student evaluations, which were mostly good, but often contained some surprises. For example, some students expressed their disappointment in the course because I hadn't done something they were expecting, like providing them study guides or teaching about a particular biology topic that I had never planned on teaching. And some students expressed anger at me or the university for making them take a general education science course, especially a course, like mine, where they had to take exams with short-answer questions. Craziness. Had I known about these issues and concerns sooner, I might have been able to make appropriate corrections and steer things differently to minimize the impact this clearly had on their willingness and motivation to learn. Because things were mostly okay, and only a handful of students expressed having difficulties, I did my best to react to the end-of-semester feedback in my planning for the next term. However, despite my efforts to respond to student feedback, I kept getting comments from a handful of students that made me pause. And then everything changed. I met the small group instructional diagnosis (SGID) technique.

The SGID is not some sort of medical procedure—although it sounds like one. My first encounter with this technique was at the University of Virginia, where they called the SGID the "Teaching Analysis Poll" (TAP). The SGID also goes by names like the "Mid-Semester Course Analysis" (MSCA, Colby College), the "Mid-Semester Interview About Teaching" (MIT, Grand Valley

State University), "Mid-Semester Group Analysis" (MSGA, University of the South), and a variety of other names. But at the end of the day all of these methods are the SGID, which is simply four conversations that you can use to solicit midsemester feedback from your students. Actually, the SGID allows you to collect amazing, actionable midsemester feedback that empowers you to make necessary midcourse corrections—small or large— to ensure you and your students experience a productive teaching and learning environment.

What did I learn from my first, second, and 20th SGID? Loads. Why? Because the SGID doesn't ask students to fill out a Likert-scale survey or jot down a few comments; it asks them to talk about how your class promotes and hinders learning with a learned colleague guiding their discussions. These conversations happen during the middle of the semester where, under the guidance of one of your colleagues, students distill their conversations into feedback they write on the board for the entire class to discuss and debate. Thus, the results come in the form of a conversation that starts with the students and ends in your office as your colleague shares with you the conversations they had with your students about the course.

Sure, I learned things from the SGID I already knew—that I talk fast (because I am from the North and most of my students were from the South) and that the textbook didn't help their learning (because there was no textbook). But I also learned that they didn't understand why we were doing some of the active learning assignments and why I had them complete warm-up quizzes before each class (how annoying of me). Thus, I was able to revisit these topics and make slight midcourse corrections to address some of their concerns about the activities and quizzes. When I made a major pedagogical change in my course, the SGID results helped me navigate a variety of issues that often come when you redesign a course. In this case, the SGID allowed me to make small midsemester corrections to the ways I was using the learning management system and larger corrections in how I was providing feedback to their weekly research assignments. The SGID also informed course corrections that I couldn't implement until the next semester, such as rethinking when I delivered lectures to complement the research the students were doing. Yes, I still had my students complete the end-of-semester evaluations, which, combined with the SGID results, provided me with a more complete view of the course. Ultimately, knowing how the course was helping and hindering student learning guided the development of meaningful course corrections that enhanced communication about course components, increased transparency about my pedagogical decisions, and improved student learning.

—Carol A. Hurney

The SGID is a consultation method developed to collect midsemester feedback from students using structured small and large group conversations (Diamond, 2004). The SGID process is a consultation experience enriched by four conversations between students, a learned colleague we refer to as the SGID consultant (to avoid confusion with too many references to instructors), and—*you*, the instructor (Figure I.1). Student feedback obtained from an SGID includes insights gleaned from conversations students have with each other in small groups about the learning happening in a course under the guidance of a consultant (SGID Conversation 1—Student & Students). The SGID consultant engages the students in a conversation about their feedback designed to seek clarity and depth regarding how the feedback provided impacts the *learning* in the course (SGID Conversation 2—Students & Consultant). Results from the small and large group conversations form the cornerstone of a conversation between the consultant and the instructor, where the consultant collaboratively discusses how the feedback provided by the students can productively inform the pedagogical approaches and strategies used by the instructor (SGID Conversation 3—Consultant & Instructor). SGID Conversation 3 often reveals midcourse corrections the instructor could implement or clarifications the instructor can make to address student concerns. Finally, the instructor closes the feedback loop with a conversation with their students about what they learned and how best to move forward in ways that enrich the learning experience (SGID Conversation 4—Instructor & Students).

We believe that having these SGID conversations during the middle of the semester changes everything—the way students think about the teaching and learning endeavor, the way instructors perceive the learning challenges of their courses, the way educational developers understand teaching and learning throughout their institution, and the quality of the institutional academic culture. Most importantly, the SGID equips the instructor with the knowledge to make midsemester course corrections that can profoundly impact the ways students navigate the course, communicate with the instructor, and realize the ways effective teaching can enhance learning.

Before we go much further, we should probably talk about what an SGID is not. The SGID is *not* a teaching evaluation method. Rather, the SGID is a method to collect student feedback. Although the line between these two ideas may seem thin, in our minds it is a crucial distinction. We do not advocate using the SGID to evaluate teaching quality or level of student learning. Instead, we believe the SGID sits firmly in the "feedback collection" category and as such, should not be used to determine teaching quality. The SGID results can most certainly be integrated into a teaching portfolio

Figure I.1. SGID conversations.

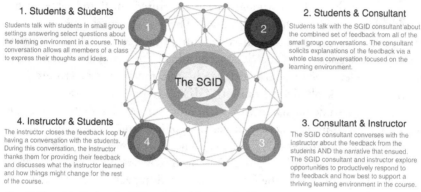

1. Students & Students

Students talk with students in small group settings answering select questions about the learning environment in a course. This conversation allows all members of a class to express their thoughts and ideas.

2. Students & Consultant

Students talk with the SGID consultant about the combined set of feedback from all of the small group conversations. The consultant solicits explanations of the feedback via a whole class conversation focused on the learning environment.

4. Instructor & Students

The instructor closes the feedback loop by having a conversation with the students. During this conversation, the instructor thanks them for providing their feedback and discusses what the instructor learned and how things might change for the rest of the course.

3. Consultant & Instructor

The SGID consultant converses with the instructor about the feedback from the students AND the narrative that ensued. The SGID consultant and instructor explore opportunities to productively respond to the feedback and how best to support a thriving learning environment in the course.

Note: © Copyright PresentationGO.com. Graphic adapted with permission.

where the instructor can reflect on the ways they responded to the results. The instructor can also integrate feedback from other sources (e.g., student evaluations of teaching [SETs], peer evaluations of teaching) in the narrative they construct reflecting on how these sources influenced their pedagogical choices and the impact these choices had on student learning.

The SGID is such a powerful midsemester course correction tool, not only because it supports the collection of rich, actionable student feedback about teaching, but also because it places a lot of value on conversations, and for good reason. Formal and informal conversations are the mechanisms by which many instructors learn about teaching. In the world of higher education, these conversations most often occur between disciplinary colleagues who have nearby offices. However, these conversations can also occur with other instructors from other departments in hallways, over lunch, at campus events, or in meetings. These conversations can involve students, mentors, and administrators. Sometimes these conversations are about teaching dilemmas the instructors are experiencing or something amazing that happened during a recent class. Sometimes these conversations are seeded with ideas from books, the scholarship of teaching and learning, or professional development workshops. Sadly, very few of these conversations are informed by constructive feedback instructors have received about their teaching.

Feedback that instructors receive from colleagues about their teaching is often limited to a few classroom observations across an entire career and focused on summative evaluations for tenure or promotion. Thus, conversations about classroom observations may not always provide insightful and actionable comments that help instructors make meaningful course corrections and reflect on the teaching and learning environment in their courses and their professional journey as educators. Thankfully, SGIDs transform the consultations instructors have about teaching into productive experiences by providing the instructor with student feedback informed by direct interaction between students and the SGID consultant and contextualized within the learning environment of that course.

Faculty also receive feedback from students in the form of end-of-semester SETs. SETs are meant to provide feedback that informs instructors on the quality of their teaching and, by extension, the learning taking place in their courses. Although there are certainly effective ways to design SETs, these instruments often do not provide the instructor with results that they can easily interpret and react to. In our roles as instructors, we have faced our own SETs and in our roles as directors of centers of teaching and learning, we have also consulted with instructors who are concerned enough about their SET scores that they have reached out to talk with us. Yet, although these consultations are important interactions, they often miss the mark of supporting effective teaching practices. Instead of talking about teaching as a primary concern, these conversations are more focused on how to get students to evaluate the course better in the future. Understandably, we would rather engage instructors in conversations about what they really care about—the quality of their teaching and how it impacts student learning. Our goal as educational developers is to help instructors become better teachers. And we want to help them use feedback from their students to do that. Yet, from our vantage points, consultations focused on SETs do not fully support a thriving culture of teaching at our institutions.

Qualitative student comments from SETs, if there are any, often emerge from the extremes of student feedback, from those who either liked or disliked the course. Often missing are comments from students with more moderate, or constructive opinions about the course. However, the qualitative feedback obtained from the SGID comes with a backstory that tells a narrative about a course—any course, in any discipline. Because it is a formative type of feedback, the SGID story is dynamic, reflecting recent and upcoming events in a course, such as project due dates and exams. The SGID provides a more complete story about a course than what is represented in the SET results or peer class observation feedback, surfacing potential differences across terms or in two sections of the same course. The SGID digs into course assessments and policies, while also exploring time spent in class and out of class, and ways the students prepare or don't prepare for class. Ultimately, the SGID is an ongoing dialogue between the students, the consultant, and the instructor connecting semester to semester, academic year to academic year, and impacting the institutional dialogue and culture around teaching.

Other methods for conducting effective instructor consultations are well documented. These approaches outline ways administrators, educational developers, and colleagues can provide robust individual consultations, mentoring, or coaching to the instructor about their teaching. Additionally, there are a myriad of peer consultation structures that institutions can provide for instructors—teaching squares, mutual mentoring groups, learning communities, or communities of practice—where they can engage in conversations about their teaching. Some of these consultation structures may incorporate opportunities for instructors to observe each other's teaching or may be focused on a specific topic or pedagogical intervention. But most often these groups talk about teaching seeded by ideas from senior instructors or the literature on teaching and learning or on ways to make teaching more manageable. They rarely take into account the perspectives of the actual learners in our courses, our current students. Again, from our collective perspectives as center directors, we value community-building experiences focused on effective teaching and learning practices and offer some of these programming opportunities for our instructors. Yet sometimes it is difficult for these conversations, whether they are one-on-one or in a group setting, to directly challenge the mental models instructors have about their own teaching and to draw inferences from student feedback, making it difficult for them to embrace substantive changes to their courses.

For the most part, instructor consultations about teaching occur one-on-one between instructors and administrators, senior instructors, or educational developers. Most of these consultations focus on performance or on a particular teaching need or topic. And most often individual consultations happen in isolation from students, who not only have insights on the factors that impact learning but would benefit from reflective conversations about teaching and learning. We believe that the SGID breaks this pattern of behavior. Instead of relying on the typical, one-to-one, isolated consultation structure most often provided by centers for teaching and learning, the SGID provides formative feedback on teaching informed by students' voices. It creates intentional conversations about the teaching and learning endeavor, which is at the heart of experiences that support effective instructor mentoring and development.

Each SGID conversation holds a promise to make teaching and learning a more transparent, collaborative, and meaningful experience. Although students often talk with other students, and instructors most certainly talk with other instructors, the SGID conversations provide a space for these players to talk openly and purposefully about teaching and learning. For these reasons, we feel that instructors and educational developers should consider implementing, expanding, or enhancing SGID conversations on their campuses.

We recently conducted a survey about SGID that included over 200 individuals who engage in educational development endeavors, which we will draw from throughout this book. Many campuses already do offer the

SGID as a midsemester course service through faculty development offices, such as centers for teaching and learning (our survey found that 60–65% of respondents have SGIDs on their campuses, but this estimate is likely higher than the true average across the United States and Canada). Yet the SGID can also be integrated into existing mentoring programs or become one of the informal opportunities instructors share with one another to enhance their teaching. Additionally, the SGID can be used to leverage campus priorities by aligning the questions posed to students during the SGID with specific teaching goals or learning initiatives.

Combined, the SGID conversations make good on a promise to enhance academic culture by intentionally connecting students, SGID consultants, and instructors with constructive feedback about teaching *and* learning. Think about this question: When do students talk with other students about how a course impacts their learning? You might have dreams that these kinds of conversations are happening at the dining hall or when students are studying, but they are probably not. And how often do students get to talk about teaching and learning with a trained consultant facilitating the discussion in productive and constructive ways? Again, not very often.

SGID conversations create memorable moments where students speak teaching and learning truths that can help support effective midsemester corrections. During the large group conversations with students, we have witnessed teaching and learning gems such as *Going to the Spanish table for lunch is one of the best ways I help my learning in this class* or *I always review my notes right after class, so that I can figure out what I missed* or *This professor really facilitates a great class discussion.* Of course we also hear students express their concerns in ways like *The TAs for this class are not well prepared to help me during office hours* or *Since the homework is due the night before class, I often procrastinate* or *I wish the professor would provide better explanations of some of the more difficult concepts we are covering; instead she just repeats what she has said in a different order.* Of course, all of these types of feedback are valuable for improving the learning environment and are especially helpful at the midsemester point, offering the chance for the instructor to make corrections to homework due dates, improve the ways they explain material, and adjust how the TAs support the course.

We have also witnessed what we call the perfect SGID moment. These moments most often happen during the large group conversation when a student is trying to explain to the SGID consultant why the amount of reading or length of an assignment is just too long or too hard and how this may be impacting their learning. The consultant attends to this student through direct eye contact and then turns to the class and asks them for their thoughts on this topic. And then it happens. A student looks at the consultant and the other student who was lamenting about the length or difficulty of an assignment and says plainly to everyone in the class—*This is college; we are supposed to be reading a lot and doing hard assignments*—or something equally poignant. Yes, this *is* college and hearing this perspective from a fellow student instead of the SGID consultant or the instructor has a profound impact on the rest of the students contemplating what we hope is a deeper understanding of the teaching and learning experience in that course, with that professor, and at that institution. The SGID brings conversations about teaching and learning home—into the classroom, often down to the level of assignments—and many times the students self-correct during the SGID. And when the instructor and students make appropriate corrections to SGID feedback, it strengthens the academic culture in that course, impacting more than just the students in that room.

Compelling conversations also emerge during the SGID consultation with the instructor. For example, students often express to the SGID consultant that they would like more clarity on assignments, especially on ways that the instructor grades assignments. In a typical consultation model, we would suggest that the instructor develop a rubric and offer students examples of excellent work. Although we know that rubrics support more efficient grading and provide a more rigorous assessment system that helps students understand assignment expectations, instructors are often reticent to use them. However, within the SGID construct, we have heard many instructors suggest to us that *I can help the students better understand my assignments if I develop a rubric* or *Maybe I should give my students examples of quality work so they can see what it is I am looking for.* Often instructors are surprised that a 30-minute conversation with their students resulted in so much helpful information, information that they had never seen before in any of their SET results. They immediately search for the best corrections they can make to respond to the SGID feedback. Faculty tell us things like *I had no idea they found this assignment so helpful* or *I would have never known that the students were so confused about the role of reading in the course.* Although comments like this may seem trivial, they represent just a glimpse into the narrative about the teaching and learning environment that the SGID consultant can provide the instructor, which informs the conversation the instructor has with the students about their feedback. And this last conversation—between instructor and students—never happens with respect to SETs. We also suspect that the SGID stimulates rich discussions among colleagues that impact course and curriculum design.

Our individual SGID stories about the impact the SGID has had on us and the teaching and learning cultures at our institutions brought us together to write this book. And although we know that many centers for teaching and learning offer SGIDs as part of their programming portfolios, we also know that there are centers that do not offer SGIDs and that there are instructors who would use this program to collect midsemester feedback if the SGID process was made more accessible to them. We also know that the SGID impacts more than just the learning environment of courses. Instructors, students, SGID consultants, and the institutional culture all benefit from the SGID experience. We believe that the SGID is so impactful, we direct significant amounts of our time engaging our efforts supporting the SGID process at our institutions. We hope to convince you that this midsemester course feedback technique is worth a first, second, or 100th look. Getting the most out of each SGID conversation is what this book is about. And although getting an SGID program up and running on a campus may seem simple, especially if the SGID is an informal process between two friendly faculty members, it is worth considering a range of situational factors around each of the four conversations. These factors, we have found through practice, can be instrumental in the success of SGIDs. Simply hoping that the SGID will have a transformative impact on students, instructors, and the campus culture will not ensure that your institution will get the most out of the experience.

Our book takes you on a journey informed by our SGID experiences, our SGID survey data, and the SGID literature. More importantly, we tell SGID stories along the way and explore interesting tangents to help place you in the lived experience of the SGID. We have written this book with a wide-ranging audience in mind. Whether you are an instructor or an educational developer, you will find yourself and your needs reflected. Additionally, this book will appeal to instructors and staff serving on faculty development committees, those associated with centers for teaching and learning (CTLs), and those with related academic administrative roles.

We begin chapter 1 of Part One, "In Search of Midcourse Correction: Discovering the SGID," by examining the core elements and complete process for the SGID—the four conversations that are the heart of the SGID and the questions you can use to seed these conversations. We continue in chapter 2 by discovering more about variations in the SGID we found in the literature or that we have implemented in our centers. In Part Two, "Getting Started," we explore the process for an instructor at an institution (chapter 3) and for a center director (chapter 4). Once you start doing SGIDs either with a group of colleagues or as a part of a CTL, Part Three, "Making the Case," examines how the SGID directly impacts a course, offering ideas for midcourse corrections and other pedagogical insights (chapter 5) and how the SGID impacts more than just the course (e.g., instructors, consultants, department culture, curriculum, academic culture; chapter 6). In Part Four, "Maximizing the Potential," we end by exploring ways to get the most out of the SGID, examining strategies we have used to improve the SGID experience and grow SGID programs (chapter 7) and how instructors and centers can use the SGID as a research tool or, better yet, engage in research addressing the many unanswered questions regarding SGIDs (chapter 8). We conclude in "Unwrapping the Promise of the SGID," with stories on the ways the SGID continues to impact our work as educational developers.

PART ONE

IN SEARCH OF MIDCOURSE CORRECTION

Discovering the SGID

THE SGID

One day during my first college teaching job, years ago, I was sharing a meal with a group of students from one of my courses. They had volunteered to provide regular feedback to me so we could alter the nature of our course as we progressed through it, engaging in some corrections as we saw fit. After a long-winded explanation for some approaches I use, one of the students chimed in with a comment that I perceived to be mixed with a bit of admiration and surprise: "You must really think a lot about teaching."

She was right. I do think a lot about teaching. And I have also been fortunate over the years to have the opportunity to speak about teaching with others and write about it in a scholarly way. About a decade later this would lead me to become the senior associate director of the Center for Teaching and Learning at Colby College, where this book you're reading took form.

I do think a lot about teaching. But here's the thing: Most teachers think a lot about teaching. Most teachers have reasons for the assignments they have designed, the ways they approach class time, and the readings they select. Most teachers think and care a lot about teaching. My student was right about me, but little did she know, she was right about almost all the teachers I have ever met.

This idea was swirling around in my brain when I sat down to give my first SGID consultation with a faculty member at Colby College on a chilly morning in October of 2018. I think a lot about teaching, but he probably does too. What makes me the "expert," particularly in his course? Why am I the one on this side of the table, not the other way around?

Then I regrouped. I wasn't coming into his office empty-handed. Just the day before I had conducted an SGID in his classroom, where some conversations ensued, and they gave me some of the most thoughtful feedback I'd ever heard about a course. His students shared with me what they found confusing, where they struggled with readings, and what they had forgotten was in the syllabus (until a neighbor reminded them). But it wasn't all bad news. They shared with me, too, how their instructor's enthusiasm for the subject was contagious, and they were surprised at how much they connected with the material, and him. They told me the truth about their course.

Before our consultation meeting, I typed up a report containing his students' ideas and constructed some key themes that described our conversation. I wasn't coming into this consultation empty-handed. I had the truth with me, at least as his students saw it. Although I find the idea that I'm some expert on teaching debatable, what's not debatable is that, at that moment, I was the expert on how his course was going for his students. Perhaps I was more of a conduit for students' ideas than an expert. In that spirit, this instructor and I proceeded to have a conversation for about an hour about what his students were seeing in their course, what ideas and corrections midway might be helpful, and how to have a frank follow-up conversation with students about what the rest of the semester could look like. We imagined the great potential the second half of this course had for his students, and developed a plan for how to realize that potential. That's the bright side of all courses. Even if they have a not-so-stellar first half, they can have a brilliant second half. And everyone will appreciate the improvements.

Was I some kind of expert, or was I some kind of conduit? Who really knows? But what this instructor and I knew was that now he had some insightful ideas about how to work with his students to refocus on the priorities of the course for the remainder of the semester. And when I left that first consultation I knew that I could rely on the SGID process to bring out the kind of feedback instructors need to do right by their students. Whether you've been teaching a long time or a short time, whether you're the director of a CTL or a first-time instructor, SGIDs will improve the learning environment for your students.

—Jordan D. Troisi

Gathering effective feedback about college courses from students doesn't require years of expertise or a prestigious title. What it does require is a willingness to have conversations with and listen to the voices of students and instructors. Succinctly, this is what the SGID process is.

We think anyone can do this, and we will call this person who gathers this information the *consultant*. But don't be intimidated by the label. We think directors or staff of CTLs can serve as consultants, and our survey data with over 200 responses show that many of them do, but we also think seasoned and new instructors can be consultants as well, and many of them do. It's a role we play, not a full-fledged job we have. And your job title and duration of experience in the classroom matter a lot less to filling this role than does your willingness to follow a decades-old process designed to elicit the real feedback—not evaluations—students want to give to improve their educational experience. For those brand new to SGID, this chapter will provide a valuable procedure and sequence for conducting a single SGID. For those already experienced with SGID, we hope to give you food for thought as we elucidate a specific approach to conducting the process based on its storied past. At times we will draw directly from approaches to conducting SGID that exist in peer-reviewed articles and the data we have from our recently collected survey of educational development professionals (including many full-time faculty members), but at other times, we will draw more from our own approach to conducting SGID in our practice and in the classrooms at our schools. With this in mind, we think this chapter has something for everyone—whether you know this topic well or not at all, whether you have a lot of SGID experience or a little, whether you've been teaching for 20 years or 2 years.

To help conceptualize the process of conducting a single SGID, we have constructed an infographic (see Figure 1.1). In a nutshell, there are six general phases to the SGID process. The first phase includes tasks that happen before the SGID classroom visit occurs, including things like scheduling the SGID session. Then during the classroom visit two conversations occur: SGID Conversation 1 (Students & Students) and SGID Conversation 2 (Students & Consultant). During these conversations the students will discuss the factors impacting their learning in the course, and the consultant will seek clarifying information from the students. After the in-class SGID session has ended, the consultant will meet with the instructor to have SGID Conversation 3 (Instructor & Consultant) and talk with the instructor about what transpired

Figure 1.1. Overall SGID process.

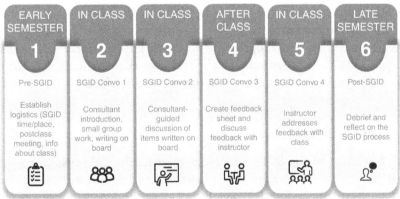

during the in-class session. After this meeting between the consultant and the instructor, the instructor will follow up with students about the nature of the feedback, which is SGID Conversation 4 (Instructor & Students). Finally, it can be helpful to engage in a post-SGID phase to provide concluding components of the overall SGID process, such as evaluation of the SGID process by the instructor(s) who took part, or some more informal debriefing session about how the process went.

Before we delve too deeply into specifics about the SGID process, we think it is worth identifying some reasonable expectations for the people involved in the process. Students can expect to provide their honest feedback about what is helping and hindering their learning in the course, to discuss this feedback with their student colleagues and the consultant, and to eventually hear back from the instructor about how the class might engage in some corrections, alterations, or reminders in light of the feedback. Students should not expect that they can identify a litany of changes in the course that will be accepted wholesale by their instructor. Instructors can expect to receive honest feedback from their students about their learning, as framed by the consultant's view of the conversation that ensued during the class. They should be open to hearing the feedback, understanding where it fits with their pedagogical goals, and making reasonable corrections to the course for the remainder of the semester, or perhaps after the semester has wrapped. Although often overlooked, we think consultants also have much to gain from the process of engaging in SGIDs. Consultants should expect to listen to students, engage students in conversations about teaching and learning, and to be a conduit for the information, rather than an all-knowing problem-solver. Consultants can form connections with colleagues, come across new pedagogical techniques, and glean a better understanding of academic culture at their institution. We will explore the potential impacts of the SGID on all involved in greater depth in later chapters.

In the following sections we will detail some specific recommendations for each phase of the SGID process. For those who are new to SGID, these sections will give you all the nuts and bolts that you need to make SGID happen, either in your courses, or at your institution more broadly.

The Pre-SGID Phase

The first phase of the SGID process involves having the consultant work with the instructor to establish SGID logistics, and familiarize the consultant with the instructor and the course at hand (see Figure 1.2). If you are serving

Figure 1.2. Early semester—The pre-SGID phase.

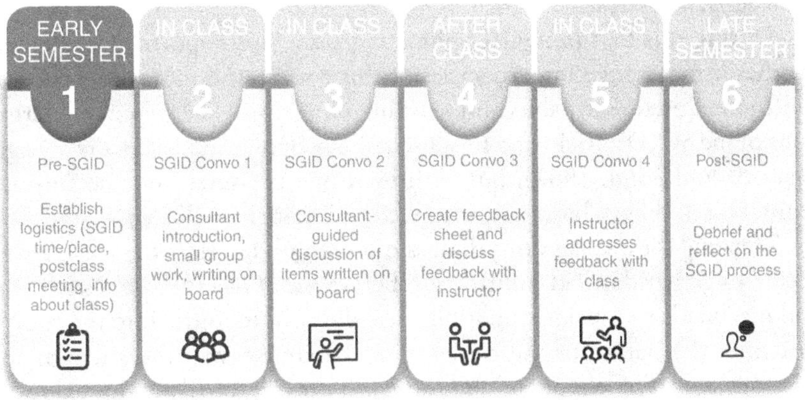

as a consultant for your friend who's an instructor down the hall or in the next building over, these steps might not require much effort, and could be done face-to-face or over email. (See Appendix B for an email template from Grand Valley State University.) But addressing these items will help you get set up to conduct SGIDs (see Table 1.1).

When should you schedule the postclass consultation? We recommend having it come soon after visiting the class. The more recently the consultant has visited the class, the more vivid memories of the classroom observation and discussion with the students will be. Having this consultation shortly after the class visit also allows the instructor to readily recall issues that may have been relevant to the class at the time of the SGID session, such as distribution of recent feedback on assigned work. The more focused the consultant and instructor's minds can be to the time

TABLE 1.1
Pre-SGID Checklist

✓ Determine where the class meets and when.
✓ Establish the precise time, during the middle of the semester, in which the SGID session will take place.
✓ Start the scheduling process for the postclass consultation with the instructor as soon after the class as possible (i.e., find available meeting times).
✓ Provide an opportunity for the instructor to share information about the course, including sharing the syllabus.

period in which the SGID took place, the easier it will be to understand the feedback about it.

During this first pre-SGID phase there are also opportunities for the instructor to describe idiosyncrasies of this course, this group of students, and the instructor's syllabus and learning objectives. The original descriptions of the SGID anticipated this discussion would occur face-to-face (e.g., Clark & Redmond, 1982), but with increased pressures on time and the proliferation of both basic and advanced technologies—like email and web conferencing—these days this discussion often occurs electronically. If you decide to gather detailed information before the SGID in-class session, we find it valuable to consider questions that allow for inquiries into the course structure, the nature of the students in the course, and the strengths of the instructor. These types of questions will provide a fairly comprehensive view of what consultants will need to know, and they also frame the SGID process as a method of identifying and leveraging strengths of the instructor and the course. The following is one example of such questions from Bowden (2004):

1. What are your goals for the class? What do you want students to do? To know? To learn?
2. What is the general atmosphere of the class?
3. How is time spent in a typical class?
4. How do you make sure the students understand what is going on?
5. Are there any questions you want to ask the students?
6. What do you think your strengths are? The class's strengths? What would you want to change? What will your students like best about the class? (p. 119)

These questions will allow the consultant to get a big picture view of the major features of the class. They also clue in the consultant on what to look for when discussing the class with the students, and in the postclass consultation with the instructor. But of course, we also recommend that these questions take a form that makes sense for the goals you have in mind for the SGID process (which may belong to you, your institution, your CTL, etc.). Many SGIDs, including the ones we lead, do not delve too deeply into this kind of discussion prior to the in-class visit. This way we enter into the conversations with few preconceived notions or expectations and little prejudice. We tend to prefer to let the SGID conversations tell the story, without a lot of framing that may alter our beliefs about how learning is occurring in the classroom.

Sidebar: At Grand Valley State University, it is standard practice to ask the instructor the following question in advance of the SGID—either via email or in person: *Are there any special concerns or areas of focus you would like me to address?* We receive a substantive response to this question in about half of the cases, but we find it useful in terms of discussing with the instructor whether or not they would like an additional question added to the SGID protocol and/or if there is a particular aspect of the course that is of concern. If an instructor is concerned about a new grading scheme or textbook choice, the consultant can either ask a specific question about this item or include a question as part of the discussion, in SGID Conversation 2. More often than not, the instructor tends to be more concerned with these matters than students are—an important result emerging from an SGID.—Christine M. Rener

Arriving in Class and Class Observation

When you arrive in the classroom for the SGID as the consultant, the first part of the process will involve observing some portion of the class (see Figure 1.3). Classroom observations are an effective way for a consultant—no matter how experienced—to understand an instructor's teaching approaches and students' responses to the instructor. When the first SGIDs were being formulated, they included a relatively lengthy classroom observation by the consultant. For example, one approach that has been taken is to have the consultant sit in on a class from its beginning, then take over and conduct the in-class SGID procedure during the last 30 minutes or so of class

Figure 1.3. SGID Conversation 1: In class.

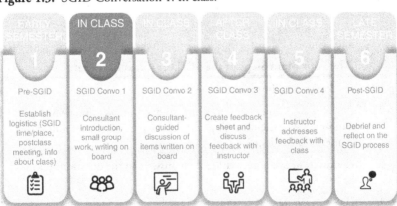

time (Redmond, 1982). Even some modern descriptions of SGIDs involve lengthy classroom observations (Payette & Brown, 2018). However, given that time is a precious commodity for most people, some might argue that the classroom observation does not have to start at the beginning of a class period, which may be 30–150 minutes before the consultant begins conversing with students and introduces the SGID process. Even a 5–10 minute chunk of class time might be enough to observe important features of the learning environment, including teacher–student rapport, the general structure of class periods, and student engagement (Ambady & Rosenthal, 1993). With regard to whether the SGID should take place at the beginning or end of the class period, we recommend that it occur at the end of the class period if possible. When it does, the instructor can introduce the consultant, then be on their way, rather than hover outside waiting for the SGID to finish. Having the SGID at the end of the class period also allows students to focus on the process, rather than other aspects of the course that might be upcoming (such as feedback on a graded work).

Consultant Introduction and SGID Conversation 1— Students & Students

After observing a portion of the instructor's course, the consultant will take over through the four major steps of the overall SGID in-class procedure, which typically take 20–30 minutes (see Table 1.2). Although 20–30 minutes may seem like a lot of time, SGID consultants will find that it goes by very quickly. Here are some more details about the four steps.

Step 1: Introduction by the Consultant

When the SGID session is about to begin, the instructor should provide a very brief introduction for the consultant—say, by name and title—and

TABLE 1.2

The Four Main Steps of the SGID In-Class Procedure

Step 1	(1–2 minutes). Introduction by the consultant.
Step 2	(5 minutes). Group work in which students answer questions on a handout about their learning and the class (SGID Conversation 1—Students & Students).
Step 3	(5 minutes). Students writing their answers to the questions on the board.
Step 4	(10–15 minutes). A consultant-guided discussion of student answers from the board (SGID Conversation 2—Students & Consultant).

then leave the room. The consultant should then provide a brief self-introduction followed by an overview of the SGID procedure within about 1–2 minutes. In order to keep this procedure brief, we have included a consultant introduction checklist (see Table 1.3). We believe that following this checklist will provide enough detail about the process for students to understand what will happen, while expediting the consultant's introduction to allow the latter portions of the SGID process to receive the lion's share of time.

Although the checklist provides a good framework for introducing the SGID, we wish to pull out three pieces here that we think deserve additional clarification. First, students are probably accustomed to end-of-semester evaluations of teaching (SETs), so pointing out how the SGID is a fundamentally different process than a SET is worthwhile. Second, mentioning that instructors' involvement in the SGID process is voluntary communicates to students that the instructor cares about their learning, at least enough to engage in the extra effort to gather student feedback at the midpoint of the semester. And third, because we have opted to include SGID questions that require students to evaluate both factors associated with the course and their own involvement in the learning process (Hurney et al.,

TABLE 1.3
SGID Consultant Introduction Checklist

✓ Consultant identifies role at institution (e.g., "professor in sociology department," "director of the CTL").

✓ Statement about how the SGID procedure allows students to provide feedback about their course at the semester midpoint, which is different from end-of-semester SETs, and opens up communication between students on the instructor.

✓ Statement describing that their instructor's involvement with the SGID process is voluntary, and as such, their teaching is not being scrutinized by some evaluative body.

✓ Statement describing how students will be asked to evaluate both factors associated with the course and their own involvement in their learning process.

✓ Statement describing how the consultant is an "outsider" to the course, not involved in other matters that have bearing for students (e.g., their reputation, their grades), and will keep their responses confidential.

✓ Brief instructions about how the SGID will work: small group discussion, board comments, discussion for the whole class, and then organizing their feedback after the class session.

2014), students should know that they are about to reflect on and verbalize their role in the learning process.

Step 2: Student Group Work to Answer Questions on a Handout About the Course (SGID Conversation 1—Students & Students)

After introducing the SGID procedure to students, the consultant should have them form small groups to work on a handout that contains a set of questions about their learning and the class. This task constitutes SGID Conversation 1 and should take about 5 minutes. Let's take a moment to discuss the size of these groups. The groups can vary in number based on class size, but having many small groups—say, two or three students in total—can create difficulties, particularly when groups will later send representatives up to the board to write their responses to the questions. We find an ideal group size to be four to six individuals, which is large enough to have the group come to reasonable consensus about the important issues in the class, but small enough to leave a reasonable amount of room when all the groups send a representative up to write on the board and to prevent social loafing among the group members when they're working together. In larger classes, the group size could be increased. We also recommend that the consultant walk around the room while the groups are working. Doing so provides three major benefits. One is that close physical proximity helps ensure that students stay on task, which can be especially important in larger classes. A second is that doing so allows the consultant to get a preview of what the students are discussing about the class for when they will discuss the class as a large group. And a third is that it ensures that students know their perspectives have been heard throughout the SGID process.

Let's return now to the form that students will complete within their small groups. Each group is asked to provide collective, written feedback to a set of questions about their learning and the course. (Students may also be curious about what will happen with the forms after they are done with them. The consultant can inform them that their collected written responses will be used for notes, but to ensure confidentiality, the instructor will not see the forms.) In between roaming the room to overhear student comments on the course, while the small groups are working, the consultant should write headings on the board that mirror the ones on the forms. Researchers and practitioners have developed a variety of formulations for the questions students will complete, which we've provided in a representative list (see Table 1.4). The table is organized chronologically. As will likely be apparent, some more recent publications on SGIDs have certainly drawn from earlier iterations of these questions.

TABLE 1.4
Examination of In-Class Questions

Number of Questions	Questions	Description of Variation From Previous Question Forms	Publication Information (Sorted by Date)
2	1. List the major strengths in this course. (What is helping you learn in the course?) Please explain briefly or give an example for each strength. 2. List changes that could be made in the course to assist you in learning. Please explain how suggested changes could be made.		Redmond (1982)
3	1. What do you like about the course? 2. What do you think needs improvement? 3. What suggestions do you have for bringing about those improvements?	Focus on "liking."	Clark and Redmond (1982)
3	1. What do you think is helping you learn? 2. What do you think is hindering your learning? 3. What specific suggestions do you have for improving learning in the classroom?	Focus on learning.	Angelo and Cross (1993)
3	1. What are the instructor's major faciliation/presentation strengths? 2. What areas of faciliation/presentation need improvement? 3. What suggestions do you have for making the improvements noted previously	Focus on instructional skills and instructor/ student interactions.	Robinson (1995)
3	1. What aspects of this course/instruction enhance your learning? 2. What aspects of this course/instruction could be improved? 3. What could you—as a student—do to make the course better for yourself, your classmates, and the lecturer?	Emphasis on (a) learning and (b) student involvement in making changes to the course.	Diamond (2004)

(Continued)

TABLE 1.4 (*Continued*)

Number of Questions	Questions	Description of Variation From Previous Question Forms	Publication Information (Sorted by Date)
2	1. List the major strengths of the course. What is the instructor now doing that is helping you improve your writing and learning? Explain briefly or give an example of each strength. 2. List changes that could be made in the course to assist you in improving your writing and learning. (Please explain how suggested changes could be made.)	Target specifically on writing, as well as learning. The questions from Redmond and Clark (1982) were altered to include *writing* as well.	Bowden (2004)
2	1. List the major strengths in this course; what is helping you learn in the course? Please explain briefly or give an example for each strength. 2. List changes that could be made in the course to assist you in learning. Please explain how suggested changes could be made.	Emphasis on learning. Prompt for explanation or example of the suggestions provided.	Finelli et al. (2008)
6	1. What helps your learning in this course? 2. What hinders your learning in this course? 3. What suggestions do you have to improve your learning in this course? 4. What are YOU doing to help your learning in this course? 5. What are YOU doing to hinder your learning in this course? 6. What could YOU be doing to improve your learning in this course?	Emphasis on learning. Requires students to reflect on their own role in their learning.	Hurney et al. (2014)
3	1. What (if anything) is interfering with your learning? (STOP) 2. What suggestions do you have to improve your learning? (START) 3. What is your instructor doing that helps you learn? (CONTINUE)	Inclusion of the behavioral instructions for the instructor.	Veeck et al. (2016)

> **Sidebar:** In the early 2000s, the SGID team at James Madison University began to notice that students were only focused on the role of the instructor when providing their feedback during the SGID. We had been using a three-question prompt that asked students to indicate what helps their learning, what hinders their learning, and what suggestions did they have to improve learning. To remedy this, we added a set of questions that directly challenged the students to reflect on their role in the course. We were immediately impressed by how the additional questions improved all of the SGID conversations. We tested the impact of these questions by designing a controlled study comparing the new learner-centered SGID with the traditional SGID (Hurney et al., 2014). Our results demonstrated that a statistically significant number of students who experienced the learner-centered SGID reported making positive changes to their study behaviors as a result of the experience. Additionally, we found that students who experienced the learner-centered SGID reported a better understanding of course assignments, more interactions with classmates, increased motivation to excel, and more enthusiasm for the course.—Carol A. Hurney

Virtually all formulations of the questions in Table 1.4 require students to list the strengths of the course or instructor, as well as changes they would suggest for the future of the course. Most of the formulations require students to emphasize aspects of the course associated with their learning specifically, rather than more superficial aspects of the course. Additionally, many of the formulations request that students offer suggested methods for bringing about improvements in the course, either about themselves or the instructor's approach to the class. Finally, some of the formulations, especially those with fewer overall questions, request that groups provide specific examples of behaviors or activities.

To us, it seems folly to pick one of these sets of questions and hold it up as the "best" version of questions to use in an SGID. Doing so would ignore meaningful priorities that may vary based on instructor goals or institution type. But in choosing the questions to use, we suggest considering three important issues.

First, these questions should focus on student learning rather than asking what students like or dislike about a course. Too often, feedback that students provide about their courses is allowed to fall into the category of preferences they have, such as how they would like to spend class time, instead of aspects of courses that have a direct impact on their learning. Indeed, end-of-semester SETs often fall into this trap, producing a compendium of what students liked or disliked, instead of a meaningful analysis of how the class helped them learn and why.

Second, these questions should direct students toward aspects of the learning environment that could be reasonably corrected during the remainder of the semester, in either the students or the course structure. Most often, effective questions have to do with behaviors that can be changed, rather than something like the disposition or personality of the instructor. Indeed, questions that prompt students to respond with answers like *The instructor is a hard grader* are less useful, and less likely to produce a change in the future of the course, than responses like *I wish the instructor provided more detailed feedback that would help us understand our grades.* To this end, questions that bring out students' and instructor behaviors, and not dispositions, are often the most valuable. Said another way, questions that get at "when," "how," and "why" are typically more useful than questions that get at "what."

Third, we think it is valuable for students to identify—write down, verbalize, and discuss—how their behavior in the course has an impact on their learning. Even as active learning has become a more common part of the teaching vernacular, it is easy for students to fall back on the idea that teachers are the dispensers of knowledge and that students are the passive recipients of it. Questions that prompt students to consider what they are doing to influence their own learning, either during class time or out of it, can change the conversation about learning altogether. They require students to acknowledge and publicly state when they are skimming through reading, procrastinating on major assignments, or relying too heavily on groupmates for collective tasks. When they tell their peers this, or hear how their peers are struggling similarly, it forces them to consider pathways they might take to more effective study and work behaviors. Psychologists have long known that committing to or publicly identifying behaviors is an important first step in behavioral change (Gollwitzer, 1999; Kiesler, 1971; Lerner & Tetlock, 1999).

Step 3: Students Write Their Responses to the Questions on the Board

Once students have completed the questions on their handout, they should send one or two students to the front of the room to write out their group's responses, verbatim, on the board under the corresponding question headings. It is important that each response get written on the board, because even something that might seem like a small issue to one group might spark an important discussion among the entire class of students.

This task should take about 5 minutes. But as any teacher could tell you, writing on the board can take a lot more time than one might expect, so bring lots of markers or chalk so that multiple students can write simultaneously. To the extent that it is possible, we recommend moving quickly through this process. This is because the next step, the consultant-led discussion of the written information with the whole class (SGID Conversation 2—Students & Consultant), is arguably the most insightful, nuanced, and dynamic component of the in-class SGID process, and you will want to save time for it. To expedite the writing process, we recommend that the consultant do what is necessary to get at least one representative from each group up to the board as soon as they have finished their question sheets (this is especially true in courses with lots of groups). One reason for doing so is simple math: If there are 12 groups, only so many representatives from each of those groups can write on the board at one time. Another reason to get students up to the board as soon as possible is that doing so sets norms for the duration of the task. If students get the impression that all the other groups are still working, then they perceive that to be the norm, and they will keep working within their individual groups, even when adding more information to the question sheets might be of minimal value. When slower working groups are getting an indication that other groups are wrapping up, these indications might move the slower working groups to wrap up in short order.

Another way to expedite the process of student writing on the board is more procedural. To this end, we recommend announcing to the students as they are approaching the board that if they see on the board a response that is the same as something their group has also written, they should simply add a checkmark by it. This saves time, and when students adhere to this instruction, it also has the added benefit of informing the consultant of the topics that seem most prominent in the class.

Another technique to keep the process moving is to start asking questions of the class as the last few students are writing on the board. In addition to this being a time-saver, it is also a valuable way for the consultant to gather information about how the class functions in what would otherwise be a time for watching and waiting. This can be done by asking a relatively simple question, such as *Tell me about the flow of the class.* Students will likely provide some overview information about the class—the nature of assignments, how class time is used, and reading length and difficulty—and this will give the consultant something to think about while students are finishing up their writing on the board. This question often provides a nice segue to the topics on the board as well.

SGID Conversation 2—Students & Consultant

The last of the in-class tasks, Step 4, involves having the consultant discuss the feedback on the board with the entire class (see Figure 1.4). We've called this *SGID Conversation 2—Students & Consultant*. This is arguably the most valuable part of the in-class protocol, and as such, it should take up the lion's share of time, ideally 10–15 minutes.

In the abstract, this process sounds rather simple: The consultant will pick out a topic written on the board—probably one that seemed to be a comment from multiple groups—and ask the class for more information, clarification, or specifics. This procedure can then be followed for the other significant issues written on the board, or ones that come up among the students during this conversation. When possible, it can be valuable for the discussion to bring out consensus on an idea or viewpoint among the students. However, we would argue that achieving consensus is not crucial. Although it is splendid when consensus emerges, reaching full or nearly full consensus within a class can be very time-consuming. We find it preferable to gather feedback on a variety of topics, rather than drilling down deep to find consensus on just one or two. It's also worth considering that although students may reach consensus on a particular idea, that idea might not be the soundest pedagogical approach—in which case, the instructor may have to walk them back from it. Lastly, attempting to reach consensus may silence the diversity of viewpoints, which is one of the benefits of using the SGID procedure.

In practice, the process of understanding the feedback from the board during Conversation 2 is aided by finesse at navigating group discussions. It involves reading, listening to students, verbalizing information, and interpreting verbal and nonverbal cues to determine the meaning of feedback, all

Figure 1.4. SGID Conversation 2: In class.

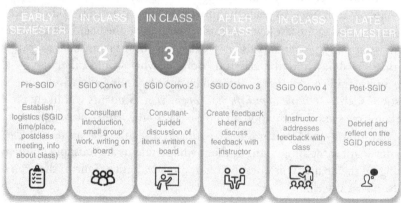

EARLY SEMESTER	IN CLASS	IN CLASS	AFTER CLASS	IN CLASS	LATE SEMESTER
1	2	3	4	5	6
Pre-SGID	SGID Convo 1	SGID Convo 2	SGID Convo 3	SGID Convo 4	Post-SGID
Establish logistics (SGID time/place, postclass meeting, info about class)	Consultant introduction, small group work, writing on board	Consultant-guided discussion of items written on board	Create feedback sheet and discuss feedback with instructor	Instructor addresses feedback with class	Debrief and reflect on the SGID process

the while thanking students for their feedback and often asking for elaboration or new topics of conversation. If you're not experienced with leading class discussions, this conversation also looks similar to conducting a focus group. Unlike other parts of the in-class SGID procedure that could follow a list or be somewhat scripted, SGID Conversation 2 is more free form. As such, we cannot tell you how it should go. But we can recommend some tips for leading this conversation effectively.

Tips for Starting and Establishing a Tone for the Conversation

- Encourage the students to talk with you by starting with something that is positive or something you suspect they would have lots to say about (e.g., exams, assignments).
- Try to create a conversational feel to the discussion. For example, repeat back to students the things you hear them say. This can provide clarification and affirms that their ideas were heard.
- Remember that you are not on anyone's side in this class—neither the students' nor the instructor's. Believe this, and act in kind. If "two sides of the story" seem to be emerging, avoid getting too much on one side of the story. Avoid promising things to the students or suggesting that things will change (although a conversation with the instructor can produce these kinds of course corrections). But do affirm that you've heard the students' views.

Tips for Drawing Out the Important Information

- Remember that this SGID conversation is designed to get the backstory on the feedback they've written. You want to get them to explain their feedback to you, so choose things that seem cryptic or things you don't understand. Vague phrases such as *more organization, more emphasis on important material,* or *consistency between classes* might warrant exploration.
- To gather more depth from students and to encourage students to reflect on their learning, follow up on their pieces of feedback with questions such as *What about the text or online modules is helping you learn? Tell me more about that.* This degree of detail rarely comes out in SETs or in other conversations with students.
- Although getting the backstory is important in an SGID, do not feel compelled to get the backstory on each line of feedback provided by the students. Some comments are rather one-dimensional or could be easily addressed. When this is the case, acknowledge that it sounds that way, and move on to the next comment.

- As in any good class discussion, don't be afraid of wait time. Give students time to process your questions and think about their collective feedback.
- When the initial discussion reaches a lull, consider asking a leading question such as *Now that you have seen all of the comments on this side of the board, does anything else come to mind? Something from your individual reflections or group discussions that isn't captured here?*
- Make sure to direct student comments to things about their learning if they are not that way already. Ensure their comments are not just preferences about what they would "like" to have happen.
- Look for feedback that shows up as the answer to multiple SGID questions. For example, if "the textbook" shows up under the headings of what helps students learn, what hinders their learning, and what suggestions they have about their learning, then ask them to explain this.
- Be careful, when trying to get an understanding of students' views, not to twist their ideas into something that is different from what they truly mean. Ask for clarification if they are sharing a complex idea, by saying, for example, *It sounds like you described . . . Am I understanding you right?*

Tips for Examining Student Agreement or Consensus

- Seek out information about how widely shared the feedback is. Occasionally ask for a show of hands to determine if a topic is relevant for large or small proportions of the class.
- Just as in any good classroom discussion, do not let a small group of students dominate the conversation. Explicitly encourage quiet groups to contribute.
- Read the room for signs of significant emotion, either verbal or nonverbal. And when it is not clear why that emotion exists, ask a probing question to understand the topic better: *It sounds like people are feeling frustrated about the large essay task, but I don't think I know enough about it to know why. If you all are feeling frustrated, can you tell me why that is? Help me understand.*
- If you are able, jot down brief notes about important pieces of the conversation that didn't end up on the board. We also think that it sends an important message to the students that their feedback is being taken seriously to see the consultant taking notes during the discussion.

Tips for Winding Down the Conversation

- As the conversation wraps up, invite students to add any feedback that they feel is important and not yet discussed, or that was prompted by the discussion.
- Finish by thanking the students for their feedback and active participation in the process.

Oh, and one last thing before leaving the classroom. Record the text of the information written on the board verbatim. Although early work in SGIDs may have required a note-taker or overhead transparencies to do this, most individuals will likely prefer the ease of taking pictures of the board with their smartphone or other device that will digitally capture the information. Also, make sure to collect all of the small group written feedback forms and either retain them in a way that maintains confidentiality or shred them. Consider traveling with fresh erasers or a stash of board wipes to ensure the board can be erased thoroughly and quickly.

Reviewing and Synthesizing the Feedback Provided by Students

After the classroom visit component of the SGID is complete, the consultant will need to compile all the information that's been gathered. Among these pieces of information are the photos taken of the information written on the board, as well as the content of the discussion between the students and the consultant. Unless a major technological error occurs, the photos aren't going anywhere, but memory of the discussion with students can fade away if not recorded promptly. As soon as possible, the consultant should write down notes from the discussion. What were the major themes of the discussion, and were these written on the board, or did the discussion veer in a different direction than some information that was written on the board? Did students' comments coalesce on particular issues—such as instructor communication, feedback processes, and so on—even if students didn't explicitly state these issues? Which aspects of the feedback resulted in the greatest divergence of student perspectives? What comments were about course aspects that could be easily adjusted within the timeframe of this course, and what comments were long-term considerations that the instructor probably can't act on now, but might save for a future redesign of this course?

Before consulting with the instructor, all of the relevant information from the in-class SGID session should be consolidated onto a feedback sheet. To make viewing the information easier, we recommend that all of the feedback fit on one organized, easy-to-read sheet of paper (see Appendix A for sample feedback sheets from Colby College and Grand Valley State University).

SGID Conversation 3—Instructor & Consultant

The consultation with instructors is an important part of the SGID process (see Figure 1.5), and one that produces better instructor and student ratings of teaching (Finelli et al., 2008; Piccinin, 1999). Engaging in this consultation should include thoughtful consideration of many factors. As such, in chapters 3 and 4 we will delve deeply into the process. But while we're moving through the steps of the SGID process, we thought it a good idea to provide some quick tips about consulting here as well, especially for those who haven't engaged in a consultation with another instructor before.

In terms of general tone, make sure to keep the approach to the consultation comfortable and supportive, especially early in the consultation process. Also make sure to communicate, explicitly and implicitly, that the feedback you provide will be kept confidential (Penny & Coe, 2004). When providing information about the SGID specifically, discuss it in general terms, such as *A topic touched on by many students was alignment between class topics and exams. . . .* Also make sure to provide a meaningful context for the information shared during the in-class SGID session, such as *Students seem to be quite interested in most of the readings, and they said so, but a few in particular gave them trouble.* With the instructor absent from the conversation, they would otherwise have no perspective on these contextual factors (Payette & Brown, 2018). During the process, it can be valuable to ask the instructor about their perspective on the feedback, including if there are factors that are surprising or if they learned anything new in the process. As the consultation is nearing its end, if not already discussed, the consultant should ask the instructor how they are planning on having a follow-up conversation with their students

Figure 1.5. SGID Conversation 3: After class.

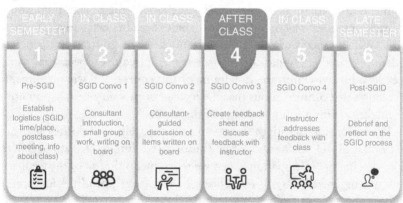

(SGID Conversation 4). Also near the end of the conversation, the consultant should hand the instructor the feedback form used to organize student feedback. Although the information contained on the form itself should be the basis for the entire consultation, instructors should have a chance to look at it and ask any questions about the information it provides. The consultant should also take the opportunity to provide contextual understanding of the information on the form, so as to prevent the instructor from agonizing over a particular comment that may or may not have had significant meaning during the in-class conversations. The consultant may also offer to role-play or go over ways in which the instructor can frame their remarks to students.

SGID Conversation 4—Instructor & Students

The instructor has the chance to close the loop of the process with students during SGID Conversation 4 (see Figure 1.6). By this point, students will have talked with one another about the course, students will have discussed the course with the consultant, and the consultant will have discussed the student feedback with the instructor. Conversation 4 allows the instructor to set the stage for what might happen for the rest of the semester with the students, perhaps more so than any other step in the process (Black, 1998; Payette & Brown, 2018). It is important for the instructor to address the major features of student feedback and discuss which midcourse corrections are feasible for the remainder of the semester because of scale or timeframe and which are not (e.g., suggesting a correction to an assignment that has already been completed). Where there appear to be discrepancies in student opinions, it can be

Figure 1.6. SGID Conversation 4: In class.

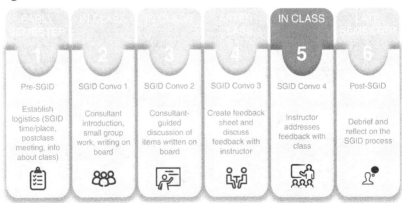

fruitful to try to resolve these through some more discussion. And, of course, if student feedback suggested significant changes or corrections that are not feasible given some significant pedagogical rationale for the instructor, it is valuable to name this and explain why.

Tips for the Instructor in Addressing the SGID Feedback With the Class

- First and foremost, thank the students for the feedback.
- Do not take a defensive stance.
- Summarize the major takeaways from the feedback.
- Address what changes are planned.
- Explain or clarify assignments/expectations, if relevant.
- Do not take too much class time and/or belabor each individual piece of feedback. The students should not be left wondering why they did the SGID in the manner in which they did if it was going to be completely rehashed in the next class period.
- Consider carefully if you will share the entirety of the student feedback.

The Post-SGID Phase

By this point the SGID process might seem about done. The SGID has been scheduled and conducted, the feedback has been collected and disseminated to the instructor, and the instructor has talked with students about that feedback. But we recommend engaging in one more step: to debrief and discuss how the SGID went (see Figure 1.7). We wanted to make clear at the end of this chapter that there is great value in finding closure about

Figure 1.7. Late semester—Post-SGID.

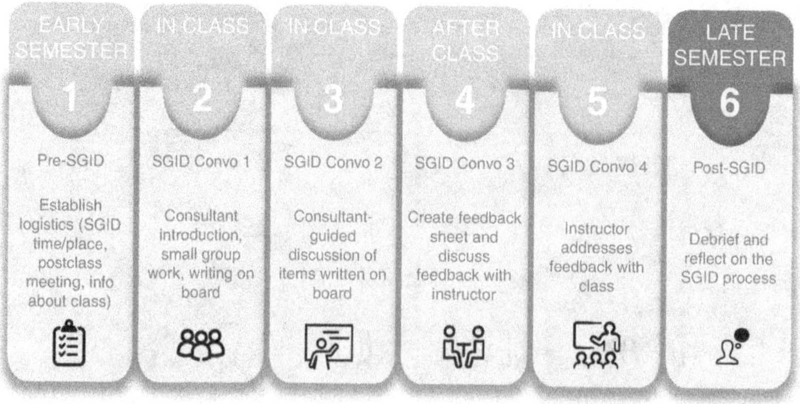

EARLY SEMESTER	IN CLASS	IN CLASS	AFTER CLASS	IN CLASS	LATE SEMESTER
1	2	3	4	5	6
Pre-SGID	SGID Convo 1	SGID Convo 2	SGID Convo 3	SGID Convo 4	Post-SGID
Establish logistics (SGID time/place, postclass meeting, info about class)	Consultant introduction, small group work, writing on board	Consultant-guided discussion of items written on board	Create feedback sheet and discuss feedback with instructor	Instructor addresses feedback with class	Debrief and reflect on the SGID process

the SGID process. And we think this is true whether you've engaged in an SGID for your colleague down the hall or if you have a large CTL with a robust SGID program. Like the other conversations that have happened along the way in the SGID process, a more conversational debrief could be the right approach: an opportunity to discuss what went well, what you would change for next time, and what are your closing thoughts. Or for those who prefer a more structured process, an evaluation form with opportunities to provide quantitative data and qualitative comments might be the way to go. But whatever route you take, don't miss this opportunity to reflect on how the process went and how it could operate in the future.

2

SGID VARIATIONS

Several years ago, I headed off to conduct an SGID for an instructor in the sciences. I was relatively new to campus and not particularly familiar with the classrooms in the building. Having met with the instructor in advance, I was aware that there were 75 students enrolled in the course. In my preparations for that day, I tossed a few extra sets of markers into one of our center's designated SGID bags (featuring our center's logo and containing a laminated introductory script card, whiteboard markers, whiteboard wipes, extra pens and paper, notebook, my cell phone, and the course syllabus) and headed toward the classroom. Well, having not checked out the room in advance, I was dismayed to find a tiered room with tables arranged in fixed rows and chairs that swiveled ever so slightly from side to side. As I sat in the back of the room, surveying this strange landscape, I noticed the vast distance between the rows of tiered tables. Would students be able turn to classmates seated behind them during the small group discussion component of the SGID? Furthermore, why were the seats in each row so far apart? With that many students talking at once, would they even be able to hear the student seated right next to them? In the few minutes before the instructor turned the class over to me, I noticed the most challenging feature of the classroom—the only whiteboard was in the very front of the lecture hall—and it was tiny. So much for the extra markers—they would not be needed.

My on-the-fly approach to engaging all 75 students in the SGID was several-fold: I increased the size of the groups to six students. Thankfully, the room was designed for 100 students, so I asked the groups to move from their seats and spread out a bit. I asked a single representative to record the group's responses on the board. As a time-saving measure, I typically ask that at least two students from each group come to the whiteboard, but in this case, there simply wasn't room. I tightened up the timing to keep things moving and to compensate for the time it took to assemble into dispersed groups. Lastly, I asked the students to gather at the front of the room and we conducted the interview conversation of the SGID with most of the students standing. It would have been virtually impossible for students to see what was written on the board if students were seated in any row beyond the first one. Thankfully, being a science lecture hall, there was ample space around the lectern/demonstration table. It all worked out fine, in part because I kept cool and acted as though this was exactly what was supposed to be happening. Suffice it say that since then, I make sure that if I am unfamiliar with the classroom, I either visit ahead of time or ask the instructor if there is anything special that I should know about the classroom—particularly *in the instances of large class SGIDs.*

—Christine M. Rener

What we have described in chapter 1 is a fairly prototypical, in-person SGID session, and one that any of us would conduct ourselves. There are types of classes, however, for which this format is either logistically challenging or simply not possible. How might you carry out an SGID in a fully online class? Or one with over 100 students? Or with an instructor who is eager to gather feedback from students but is not willing to devote the class time required for an SGID? Overcoming such obstacles is possible by expanding your SGID options to include some of the variations explored in this chapter. You might also consider the possibility of student-led SGIDs. Ultimately, the SGID format you select can be modified to align with the long-term goals you have as an instructor, as a department, or as a CTL. And indeed, the over 200 respondents to our survey about SGID practices indicated that on many campuses, despite an abiding appreciation for the value of all forms of midsemester feedback, time and personnel constraints have led individuals and offices to either adapt SGID procedures or take nuanced approaches. We encourage you to experiment with SGID variations and determine the best fit for you, your colleagues, your center, and institutional culture.

Some of the alternative SGID formats have been informed by concerns about the time commitment involved on the part of the instructor, the consultant, or both. As a relatively structured, multistep process, the SGID can be more time-intensive for both instructors and consultants than other methods of gathering midsemester feedback. Of our survey respondents who don't conduct SGIDs, about 25% of them felt that they don't have sufficient time to do them. Although we are committed to offering traditional-format SGIDs on our campuses, we also completely understand those interested in taking modified approaches in their institutional contexts. In dipping our toes into SGIDs in our own classrooms as well as developing full-fledged campus SGID programs, it has been helpful to carefully consider each of the steps in the SGID with respect to time commitment. As you approach SGID endeavors in your own institutional context, there may be steps that warrant streamlining or compressing and those that benefit from systematic engagement and a slower pace.

> **Sidebar:** Instructors almost never feel that the amount of class time they have is enough. We've been working with instructors for decades, and we can take this point as a given. To many, giving up 30, 20, or even 5 minutes seems like too big of a sacrifice of content they would cover. We want to push back on this idea a bit. Yes, you could cover an additional one or two concepts during that time, but as learning scientists would tell you, just "covering" material is not the same as students learning material. Gathering student feedback using SGID allows students an opportunity to engage in metacognitive reflection on their learning in a course, either solidifying where their learning is working or discovering areas where they're falling short. And it clues instructors in, too, to the sometimes surprising areas where students are really getting it, or really not getting it. We would argue that even though the SGID process may take 20–30 minutes away from the normal business of class time, it doesn't subtract from learning; it adds to it. And our feedback from instructors corroborates this perspective. They point out that SGIDs help them figure out how to focus their class time, provide concrete instructions for assignments, and improve communication with students for the remainder of the term. SGIDs may take a little bit of class time, but it's time well spent.—Jordan D. Troisi

We address issues of the time commitment in chapter 7 by discussing more thoroughly approaches to organizational structures that make the most efficient use of everyone's time, from the program coordinator to each individual consultant. We also explore in greater depth the capacity concerns around qualified consultants that were also raised through our SGID survey and provide examples of consultant training programs that can be adopted either by groups of committed instructors, departments, or CTLs. As we hope is apparent to the readers of this book, the richness of the feedback as well as the long-lasting benefits for all involved are significant enough to warrant the investment.

In the rest of this chapter, we detail several categories of common SGID variations that make creative use of class time and/or learning management systems, survey tools, and polling applications. We encourage the reader to consider ways in which these alternative approaches might be adapted to fit their particular campus contexts and constraints. Broadly speaking, the SGID variations are categorized as

- time-saving formats—minimizing use of class time
- online courses—synchronous or asynchronous strategies
- large-class strategies—low-tech or technology-mediated
- student-led SGIDs—undergraduate or graduate students as consultants

Time-Saving Formats

As relatively experienced consultants, we estimate that an SGID requires approximately 2 hours of our time as consultants. Admittedly, concerns regarding time primarily come from faculty and center on allocation of class time. On our campuses, we publicize that the SGID requires 20–30 minutes of class time. In practice, this amount does vary and is tailored slightly to account for factors such as the following:

- instructor characteristics (familiarity with the SGID process, extent of teaching experience, personality)
- consultant characteristics (level of SGID experience, educational development background, instructional consultation experience, personality)
- course characteristics (number of students, level of course)
- physical space (layout of whiteboards and computer station, seating arrangement)
- the extent of any requested class observation adjacent to SGID (during the preclass consultation, the instructor and consultant may arrange for a class observation lasting anywhere from several minutes in length to an entire class period)

In an effort to minimize the impact of the SGID on actual class time, a number of modified SGID protocols have been developed. For example, Millis and Vazquez (2010) have designed what they call the "Quick Course Diagnosis" to save time when the consultant visits the classroom. In this procedure, consultants who visit a class ask students to rate their satisfaction with their course from 1 to 5, and write a word or short phrase to clarify their experience. Afterward, the consultant forms the students into groups of five to seven to engage in a roundtable brainstorming technique where students list other strengths and weaknesses of the course. These are then compiled and grouped by theme. This process is designed to take about 15 minutes of class time, or about half the time of a normal SGID.

Another approach, the "Two Survey Method" (Finelli et al., 2011), is also designed to minimize the amount of time the instructor is removed from their role as teacher in the classroom. In this method, students respond to an initial survey outside of class and then to a second more focused survey during a subsequent class session. The second survey is informed by student responses to the first survey as well as a consultant class observation and an intermediate instructor conversation. Although it involves many steps in its own right—initial survey design, classroom observation by a consultant, collaborative development of the second survey, in-class surveying, and consultant report preparation—it has the advantage that only 7–10 minutes of class time is required to administer the second in-class survey. The quick course diagnosis and two-survey method might be particularly useful if you have instructors that feel they simply cannot sacrifice the precious minutes of their class time.

One additional time-saving procedure is worth mentioning, and it can also be especially valuable for institutions that do not have sufficient staff trained to be teaching consultants. The "Bare Bones Questions" (BBQ) method (Snooks et al., 2004) leverages the capability of "empathic colleagues" to conduct midsemester feedback sessions (see also Craig, 2007). Quite similar to an SGID, this technique uses the same questions during the in-class consultation, but does not include a conversation before the class or time spent observing the colleague's class. Instructors are cultivated as consultants via a three-step process in which instructors first observe a BBQ conducted by an experienced consultant, then experience the BBQ in their own course, and finally conduct a BBQ for a colleague. In this case, the developmental iterations of the BBQ sought to maintain the face-to-face consultant–student conversation most important to the study's authors in their institutional context.

Online Courses

Some respondents to our recent SGID survey suggested that SGIDs were not an option for faculty teaching online or cited concerns such as low response rates or student anonymity for online SGID variants. Fortunately, SGID procedures have been adapted to fit online courses in both synchronous and asynchronous ways. Most of these procedures leverage technologies such as video conferencing, online collaborative documents, or learning management systems. For example, in the "eSGID Process" (O'Neal-Hixon et al.,

2017), synchronous, 15-minute video conference conversations are scheduled with small groups of students and the consultant, each group having a designated student note-taker. The consultant then meets with the group of note-takers to review the compiled notes, ask clarifying questions, and collaboratively prepare a final report for the instructor. In another approach, students shared their midsemester perspectives simultaneously in a Google Doc, much like they would in an in-person classroom (Veeck et al., 2016). After piloting a whole class collaborative document approach, the authors elected to subdivide the class into smaller groups of students, easing the collaborative writing process. Learning management systems used by many institutions offer additional tools that could be used to record students' responses to the SGID questions (private or public journals, small group or whole class discussion boards) as well as communication tools to mediate synchronous consultant–student conversations (video, audio, or written chat). A common thread through online SGID approaches is the need to prepare the students for engaging with such feedback processes; the technology may be new or the opportunity to collaborate with their classmates in real-time authorship may require that ground rules be established and opportunities provided for students to practice (Crow et al., 2008; Payette & Brown, 2018; Veeck et al., 2016).

Large Classes

Although the threshold for considering a class to be large can be debated, we acknowledge that class size has a definite impact on the process of the SGID. Evidence also suggests that the student feedback from the SGID varies with class size, with smaller classes being perceived as more organized than larger classes (Blue et al., 2014). In terms of conducting a large class SGID, the main considerations—as exemplified in the story at the beginning of this chapter—are the number of simultaneous small group conversations, the ability to rapidly and thoroughly record items on a whiteboard (or two), and the facility with which a consultant can conduct Conversation 2 (the discussion between the students and the consultant of the feedback written on the board). For starters, a consultant can simply increase the size of the small groups and ask the students to record their notes on the whiteboard as quickly as possible, all in the service of conducting the remainder of the SGID in an unhurried and thorough manner.

Other relatively simple strategies for approaching an SGID in a large enrollment course include assigning two SGID consultants per class to help manage the data collection from the students, limiting the number of responses each group provides, or even dismissing the majority of the students at the conclusion of Conversation 1 and conducting Conversation 2 with only representatives from the small groups (Black, 1998). In a slightly more involved alternative process, you can split the student conversations of the SGID over two class periods (Black, 1998). In the first class period, the consultant introduces the SGID, students work in small groups to generate answers to the SGID questions, and students' written responses are collected. The consultant then analyzes the responses, coming back the next class period for Conversation 2, wherein the students discuss the summary prepared by the consultant.

For the more technology-savvy consultant, survey tools and polling applications can be particularly useful in large classes in quickly gathering student comments and/or capturing consensus perceptions. Such approaches do necessitate that students are alerted beforehand to bring a device to class and that the consultant is sufficiently adept with the tools. We recently learned of a process wherein the SGID consultant records small group report-out results in real time directly into a Qualtrics survey template (G. Wentzell, personal communication, November 14, 2019). The consensus-building and clarifying conversation is then hastened by prompting students to complete the survey on their own device, recording their level of agreement with the list of items using a Likert-scale system. The survey also includes an open-ended option for noting additional observations/suggestions. One can envision carrying out a similar process with any of the widely available polling websites or student response systems.

The Student-Led SGID

The final variation of the SGID as presented in chapter 1 to which we would like to draw your attention involves the nature of the consultant. Respondents to our SGID practices survey cited lack of consultant availability or uncertain consultant training protocols as barriers to SGID program development or expansion. Consultant training practices will be addressed in a subsequent chapter, but it is worth mentioning in the context of SGID variations how a number of institutions have expanded the conception of who serves as SGID consultant. These institutions have incorporated the student voice in an even more intentional way during the SGID by employing students as SGID consultants (e.g., Brigham Young University's Students Consulting on Teaching [SCOT] or the University of Michigan Midterm Student Feedback [MSF] programs). Undergraduate or graduate students are vetted, trained— with either a short orientation or a semester-long course—and supervised by pedagogical experts within a CTL (Cox & Sorenson, 2000; Wright et al., 2015). Although these students themselves may not be experts in teaching, they are able to gather and share formative feedback and have the important vantage point of being students themselves and offering the participating faculty a unique type of Conversation 3 (the consultant discussion of feedback with the instructor). Others have noted the challenges with this model in terms of shared responsibility, elevation of consultant voice, and power dynamic that is rather different than instructor–instructor or staff–instructor SGIDs (Cook-Sather, 2009). We encourage our readers considering engaging students as consultants to carefully consider the ways in which consultants are trained—again, this topic will be covered in greater detail in a subsequent chapter—and the ways in which the SGID process is framed for the instructors. Greater clarity around expectations on both sides can only be of benefit. And as one survey respondent reported, in the system on their campus that allows instructors to request either an undergraduate, graduate, or faculty SGID consultant, many instructors request an undergraduate student. What is particularly attractive to us is the potential gains for the student consultant themselves—a view under the hood of instructors and courses.

Prioritizing SGID Conversations

Which of the four SGID conversations do you consider to be the most important? The initial conversation among small groups of students? The subsequent class conversation facilitated by the consultant? The debrief conversation between the consultant and instructor? Or the follow-up conversation between the instructor and their students? Okay, that may have been a trick question—they are all important—but as you consider tweaking the format and/or timing of these conversations, it is worth considering which *aspects* of the conversations are the most important to preserve. Although moving the consultant–instructor conversations to email or phone seems a reasonable modification of the standard SGID, maintaining the integrity and depth of the student-facing phases of the SGID should take priority.

To what extent can (or should) the student–student small group conversation either be abbreviated, take place asynchronously, or even be conducted virtually? The same question can be asked of the consultant–student conversation and, of course, the instructor–student debrief. We believe that there is great value in the ability to engage all members of the class simultaneously. We also find the student conversations greatly enriched by the ability to read body language, respond to facial expressions, and notice and bring out quiet voices. If one views the SGID as being *for* the students, then the conversations *about* learning are the lodestar of the SGID. Keeping in mind our perspectives as well as the priorities of your own SGID efforts, there are a number of common SGID variations to consider.

PART TWO

GETTING STARTED

3

INSTRUCTOR-TO-
INSTRUCTOR SGIDS

Early in my faculty career, I convinced a group of biology faculty at James Madison University that we should do SGIDs in each other's classes. We were each teaching one section of introductory biology for nonmajors, which typically enrolled about 60–75 students per section, and met weekly to talk about this course and share teaching ideas. In effect, we were a faculty learning community pushing at ways to support student learning in a large-enrollment, introductory general education course. I had just learned how to do SGIDs while working at the teaching center at the University of Virginia and was eager to welcome my faculty colleagues into the magical world of the SGID. Once they agreed to give this a try, I described the SGID process to them and set up a round-robin type schedule where I did an SGID for faculty member A, faculty member A did an SGID for faculty member B, and so forth. We didn't do any formal SGID training, but we did agree to keep the information confidential within the SGID pairs and to only share out what we felt comfortable sharing with our group.

When we finished our work as the SGID consultant, we met with the instructor to discuss their results. Once we completed all five SGIDs, we brought our SGID results to the group meeting and shared what we learned from our colleague about the feedback our students provided. This instructor-to-instructor SGID experience provided each of us with direct feedback about our courses and helped us determine some midsemester course corrections that we could work on, individually and collectively, to improve the course across all sections. For example, we learned how some of us were using active learning strategies and then spent a few meetings devising ways to implement more of these kinds of experiences in all of our courses. We also realized that we needed to change the narrative surrounding this course so that students could see how this course was relevant to their lives. And the SGID opened the window for us to make this correction immediately. As a result, my end-of-semester evaluations didn't include as many comments raging against the need to take a required general education science course.

We also learned that we were each struggling trying to meet one of the common student learning outcomes for the course. As a result of this instructor-to-instructor SGID experience, we spent the next few weeks developing a project suitable for our student population and class size that we deployed that term—a major midcourse correction that proved so successful, I continue to use aspects of it whenever I teach a nonmajors course.

Ultimately, we each shared all of the nitty-gritty details of the SGID feedback with each other, even the parts that criticized aspects of our teaching or some strategy we were using. The sharing part of this process helped each of us realize that we were not the only instructor experiencing similar challenges or roadblocks in our teaching. Most importantly, this SGID experience created a sense of belonging and camaraderie within our group that fueled the excitement we all had about teaching this course. The midcourse corrections that emerged from our collective SGID experience were grounded in the student perspective of the learning environment and our shared experiences teaching this course.

We kept doing SGIDs in each other's classes over the coming years, firmly planting and germinating the SGID seed in me and in these instructors. Subsequently, some of them joined the SGID consultant team I was building in the emerging faculty development center I helped launch. And although I certainly value SGIDs run by center professionals, nothing, in my mind, beats the kind of excitement and impact of SGIDs done for faculty, by faculty.

—*Carol A. Hurney*

Instructor-to-instructor SGIDs are SGIDs that instructors set up with colleagues from within or outside their departments. These SGIDs retain all four essential conversations seeded by any of the SGID question sets described in chapter 1 (Figure 1.1). However, instructors who are doing SGIDs in other instructors' courses can integrate course-specific questions into SGID Conversation 1 that probe, more directly, aspects of the course they want students to reflect on during the SGID. Instructor-to-instructor SGIDs could also be integrated into faculty learning communities, like Carol's group of biology colleagues, where all participants agree to engage in the SGID process by serving as SGID consultants for other members of the community. We could end this chapter here, because doing SGIDs with a colleague is as easy as it sounds. The steps outlined in chapter 1 provide a running start, but to ensure a successful launch we offer a few additional insights that will support a smooth SGID experience for the consultant, instructors, and students. Specifically, we discuss ways to establish expectations of the SGID experience, ensure that SGID consultants create a positive SGID experience for both the students and instructor, and how instructors can make the most out of the SGID results.

Sidebar: Sometimes instructors want the SGID to answer very specific questions they have about their course or assignments. Although the SGID questions can be modified to ask about specific course details, I find it better to have the students express what is on their minds, rather than seeding them with questions that may seem important but may mask some of the more pressing course corrections that would be revealed by asking the broader SGID questions focused on learning in general. Typically, I tell instructors that if they still have more specific questions that the SGID did not address, the process of the SGID started a conversation with their students which the instructors can use to ask follow-up questions during the post-SGID conversations with their students.—Carol A. Hurney

---

SGID Expectations

As we discussed in chapter 1, instructors, students, and SGID consultants should expect the SGID to offer the opportunity to engage in open and productive conversations about the teaching and learning environment in a course. Specifically, instructors should expect to receive actionable feedback that may inform midsemester course corrections and students should expect to be given the space to voice their perspectives to the consultant, who should expect to be a conduit of information that supports the learning endeavor. In addition to these fundamental expectations, all participants should expect the SGID to be a confidential, formative feedback experience, where both students and faculty authentically examine ways that they could improve the learning of course outcomes. Instructors acting as the consultant for the SGID should only share information about the SGID experience with the course instructor, shred all forms that the students use to write down their feedback, refrain from discussing the SGID experience in committees that are evaluating the instructor, and be a bit elusive when colleagues (or administrators) ask why they are waiting in the hall to enter the classroom (we offer more insights into the confidentiality issue in chapter 4). The consultant should also protect the confidentiality of the students by letting them know that only their aggregate feedback will be discussed with the instructor and the

consultant will not connect feedback to any one student. Often the consultant knows a few of the students in the SGID, and if so, they should state that
although they know some of the students, they will not reveal any identifying
information to the instructor during the SGID debrief.

It's also important for the consultants to consider the power dynamics
that might exist between them and the course instructors, related to factors such as tenure status, seniority, and aspects of individual identity (e.g.,
gender, race). These dynamics can inform how to interpret and convey
feedback, and they can increase concerns associated with confidentiality
as well. Another important expectation to solidify when setting up SGIDs
is to ensure voluntary participation and not participation based on coer-
cion. In the world of instructor-to-instructor SGIDs, this may be assumed,
especially when the two instructors setting up the SGIDs mutually agree
to use this feedback strategy. However, we caution that this line can be
easily crossed, leading to situations where a department chair asks a senior
faculty to set up SGIDs with junior faculty under the auspice of helping
the junior faculty manage teaching expectations. Or junior faculty feeling
pressured to engage in SGIDs from colleagues outside their departments,
even though they are not ready to welcome the kind of feedback provided
by the SGID.

The primary goal of the SGID is to provide formative feedback to
instructors, which they can use to reflect on their teaching. Additionally,
placing the SGID in the middle of the semester creates the opportunity for
the instructor to act on the SGID feedback during that semester by making targeted corrections to address the issues revealed through the SGID
process. If the feedback is not actionable, instructors have the opportunity to continue the dialogue started by the SGID with their students by
offering insights as to why some of their feedback would not support the
desired learning outcomes of the course. Therefore, instructors should not
be required or strongly encouraged by administrators or colleagues to participate in the SGID. Similarly, faculty teaching committees or tenure and
promotion committees should not require instructors to utilize the SGID
in their courses as a means of documenting teaching excellence. Having
an SGID done in a course may indicate that an instructor is interested in
receiving *and* reacting to SGID feedback, determining whether the instructor reacted appropriately to the feedback is much harder to gauge. Aligning
with this SGID expectation avoids providing feedback to instructors who
may not welcome either the process or the product of the SGID and com-
promise the value of the feedback process. Buyers beware—make sure all
instructors consent before engaging in the SGID conversations.

Finally, although the title of this book supports the role of SGIDs in making midsemester course corrections, setting up the SGID to provide feedback that leads to major changes in a course may undercut other ways the SGID can support a thriving academic culture. In fact, promising change to faculty or students may set the SGID up for failure. Thus, prior to starting an SGID, especially instructor-to-instructor SGIDs, the consultant should explain that the SGID is not a comprehensive evaluation of teaching nor is it a formal course evaluation. Instead, the SGID is a feedback loop that provides a snapshot of the learning successes and challenges in a course from the students' perspective that are forefront in their minds at that particular point of the semester. Results from the SGID inform the pedagogical content knowledge of the instructor, often, but not always, leading to transformative midsemester course corrections.

Sometimes SGID feedback provides the exact information an instructor is looking for, but sometimes the students provide feedback on parts of the course that are not forefront in the instructor's mind. Thus, instructors must be primed to expect the unexpected and to be left questioning some aspects of the teaching and learning environment of their courses. SGID feedback provided by students is context dependent and is influenced by a variety of factors. For example, the kind of feedback provided during an SGID will be influenced if the SGID happened right before a major assignment or right after getting back graded papers or exams. However, if students have not received any graded feedback before the SGID, they are often unable to critically reflect on the ways that teaching methods, assignments, and feedback on their work support their learning and thus have little to offer in an SGID experience.

As we discussed earlier, students are very eager to offer their midsemester perspectives on a course and although the consultant clarifies that the SGID is not a guarantee of change, it does certainly open up the opportunity for things to improve, even in small ways. However, if the professor receiving the SGID is not fully onboard with the formative nature of the SGID feedback process, the SGID may do more harm than good. For example, if the instructor fails to follow up with their students about the SGID results, students may respond by feeling that their ideas were not heard. Students may also react negatively to the SGID feedback process if their instructors prove to be defensive about the feedback they offered. For these reasons, instructors and instructors serving as consultants should review the key elements of the "four conversations" we present in chapter 1 and be ready to *lean in* to the SGID results, modeling for students how to thoughtfully react to constructive feedback.

Sidebar: If I had to boil down into one sentence the advice I might provide to instructors who are considering signing on for their first SGID, I suppose it would be: "Be prepared for honesty, and be prepared to be honest." Like any process of receiving and giving feedback, this maxim captures the importance of numerous processes associated with the SGID. First, instructors should be prepared for honesty. They should be prepared for honest feedback from their students and honest feedback from their consultant colleague (although the consultant will, hopefully, not be too cruel in how they might deliver bad news). Although almost every instructor has reasons for making pedagogical choice A, B, or C, sometimes these choices miss the mark. Try to avoid being defensive when feedback doesn't go your way. After all, the students, consultant, and instructor alike all want the same thing in this circumstance: a course that fosters better and more engaging learning. Second, instructors should be prepared to be honest with the consultant and their students. Be honest about what you've tried and what might or might not be working. Be honest with your students: What changes can they expect you to make in the course and how can your students provide friendly reminders of those changes in case you forget? And be honest with your students, too, about what changes are not very realistic for the course for the remainder of the semester. Some suggestions for courses are too substantial to make at the midsemester point, so acknowledge their good suggestion, and tell them that their friends will be the beneficiaries of their thoughtful contributions in semesters to come.—Jordan D. Troisi

SGID Consultants

The SGID consultant is a complex role that we explore in more detail in chapters 4 and 7. Consultant training should be an essential part of an SGID program offered by a CTL. And although it would be nice if instructors doing SGIDs for their colleagues had some formalized training, it is not required for this kind of informal SGID experience. However, we would like to offer three guiding principles for the SGID conversations to ensure that the SGID fully reflects the student perspectives in ways that challenge the instructor to reflect and modify their instructional approaches to support the kind of learning they pursue for their students.

Principle 1

Be impartial. The consultant should not take sides during the conversations with the students or the instructor. As the students begin discussing their feedback in the small groups and then writing their ideas on the board for discussion, the consultant starts to build a picture of the class—its strengths and weaknesses. And because the consultant knows the instructor, they will be adding this new information onto what they already know about the course. Often, there are discrepancies between the two views of the course, resulting in the consultant feeling torn about which version is the right version. In fact, this probably happens in all SGIDs, even if the consultant doesn't know the instructor or the course very well. The consultant should not use the SGID conversation (SGID Conversation 2, if you are keeping score) as a teachable moment; trying to convince the students that their professor is using effective pedagogical approaches is not the consultant's job. Similarly, the consultant should not try to advocate for the student position when discussing the results with the instructor. Instead, the consultant should do their best to accurately reflect the conversation they had with the students so that the instructor has the full picture when considering any midcourse or other kinds of pedagogical corrections.

Principle 2

Foster learning-focused conversations. Sometimes the feedback students offer does not impact learning or is something the instructor does not control, such as time of the class. Other times the students want the instructor to implement one of their suggestions that may not improve learning. The desire to solve problems often clouds the primary role of the SGID consultant to foster conversations among and with students. The SGID consultant is not meant to fix the pedagogical issues raised during the SGID conversations. Rather, the SGID consultant is there to listen to the students, seek further explanation about things that the consultant doesn't fully understand, and to ensure that the conversation is focused on how the feedback offered by the students impacts their learning. Thus, conversations about the particular kinds of ties the professor wears or the final exam schedule that is set by the university are off limits (all true stories, by the way). The consultant should also encourage students to explain their feedback to each other, especially when there are differing opinions.

Principle 3

Explore meaningful course corrections. The term *consultant* might send the message to the SGID consultant that they should be pedagogical experts and able to offer effective advice to the instructor regarding the SGID results. Thankfully, SGID consultants do not have to be pedagogical experts. Instead, they should be teacher-scholars who are reflective practitioners about their own teaching and curious about what teaching looks like in other classes. After the in-class portion of the SGID concludes, the consultant should gather the student feedback from the board and then spend a few moments jotting down the themes of the discussion with the students. When the consultant meets with the instructor, they should bring a hard copy of the SGID results that includes the themes of the student conversation. The SGID consultant should start the discussion by indicating that the instructor will get the copy of the SGID results at the end of the consultation. In our experience, once you give the instructor their results, they can't focus on the conversation with the consultant. During SGID Conversation 3, the consultant should convey to the instructor the feedback offered by the students, allowing the instructor multiple opportunities to ask questions and offer suggestions for course corrections. It is totally appropriate for the consultant to offer ideas for course corrections, being mindful that the instructor may or may not decide to adopt these ideas. Finally, the SGID consultant should ask the instructor what they plan on saying to the students during the next class period, allowing the instructor to synthesize elements of the consultation into actionable steps that the instructor can convey to the students. It is not the SGID consultant's job to ensure that the instructor "fix" everything as a result of the SGID. In fact, it is okay for the instructor to realize that some things cannot be easily fixed or that the fix is best implemented in the next iteration of the course. The sample scenarios described in the next section help to further contextualize the role of the SGID consultant in the analysis and communication of the feedback provided by the students.

SGID Results

SGID results are as unique as the courses and students from which they emanate. As such, we can't provide a set of SGID results that represents a particular class format (lecture vs. discussion) or disciplinary area (Blue et al., 2014; Coffman, 1998; Heppner & Johnston, 1994). And as we have mentioned before, because the SGID provides a snapshot of student feedback about a course, SGID results may vary for a particular course and instructor based on the timing of the SGID. If the students just took an exam, there will be many comments about the exam. If you just returned graded papers to the students, then the consultant will hear about that experience. It is especially valuable to not get hung up on the "most recent event" in the class. The consultant can acknowledge it, make sure they understand it, but be sure to get back to the broader feedback from the students. The goal is to push the students to think more comprehensively about a course, revealing the themes that are most important to their learning.

Given all of this, we feel it is important to showcase mock-SGID results that reflect the kinds of results we have experienced. For each set of results, we contextualize the feedback with details about the institution, course, and instructor. We then provide the SGID results—what the student groups wrote on the board (after SGID Conversation 1) and the themes noted by the SGID consultant when consulting with the instructor (revealed during SGID Conversation 2). Finally, we examine the midcourse corrections the instructors implemented based on the SGID conversations (reflections from SGID Conversation 3).

SGID Sample Results—Susan/Introductory Chemistry

Susan is a tenure-track faculty member at a midsized research-intensive university, where she teaches introductory chemistry to 65 students in a traditional lecture hall setting. Susan is in the early years of her teaching career and wants to demonstrate that she is a reflective teacher in her evaluation materials. One of her other colleagues, Nikki, also wants to do the same. After attending a workshop offered by the CTL on midsemester feedback methods, Susan and Nikki decided to try the SGID in each other's classes. To minimize the amount of class time used for the SGID, they decided to omit the learner-centered questions we presented in chapter 1 and opted for the following three-question set: *What helps your learning in this course? What hinders your learning in this course? What suggestions do you have to improve learning in this course?*

At face value, the SGID feedback Susan's students wrote on the board suggested that some of her students thought the textbook helped their learning, whereas others thought the textbook hindered learning. The students also thought they should be going to office hours earlier in the semester, but that office hours were not at a good time for some students. Finally, Susan's students indicated that they didn't have some of the basic chemistry skills and would like more review on the basics (see Table 3.1). The results also indicate that Susan responded quickly to student emails and explained things well using the board and slides. However, some bits of the SGID results begged for more explanation, such as their comments about problem sets and the connection between class content and the problem sets. Plus, it was hard to know what the real issue was with the textbook, why students waited to attend office hours, and which basic chemistry skills they were lacking.

Nikki started the in-class conversation with the students (SGID Conversation 2) by asking them to explain why the textbook helped, but also hindered learning. After a bit of embarrassed laughter, the students told her that it wasn't the textbook that helped or hindered learning; it was

TABLE 3.1
SGID—Sample Results 1

Susan—Chem 101		
What Helps Your Learning in This Course?	*What Hinders Your Learning in This Course?*	*What Suggestions Do You Have to Improve Your Learning in This Course?*
• chalkboard notes • office hours • the textbook • quick response to emails • open to helping • explanations of PowerPoint and class notes on the board (easy to follow)	• don't have basic chem skills • the textbook • only some problems seem related to what we are learning in class • unclear connections between notes and slides—sometimes • office hours not at a convenient time for when homework is assigned	• reviewing basic chem • post slides earlier • additional office hours • go to office hours sooner • post problem sets earlier • more explanation about how class notes relate to slides • put some words on the slides • access to optional practice problems • make questions more clear/specific • tell us what we are going to focus on during each class—specific chapters/topics • be more direct about the key points and big picture of each lesson

because their professor (Susan) was lecturing on topics from the textbook they weren't reading in advance of class. Instead, they were going back after class and reading about the parts that they found confusing during class. Nikki asked how many students were doing this kind of reading and most of the students raised their hands in agreement. She followed up by asking them if this was working—was the reading helping them learn even if they did the readings after class? Most of the students indicated that it was working, but suggested that they would still like some clarity on what they could be getting out of the readings if Susan wanted them to complete the readings before each lecture.

Nikki next asked the students to explain how the problem sets differed from what was being taught during class. This conversation included some discussion of office hours. The students expressed that it wasn't that the problems didn't relate to class material at all; instead, they expressed that the problem sets were *much* more difficult than the problems and content they were learning during lectures. Even so, some students found working on the problem sets to be helpful, but because Susan's office hours were on the day the problem sets were due, many of the students could not attend these hours to get extra help because they had to attend other classes. Also, having the problem sets due on the same day as office hours resulted in many students procrastinating, because they knew that they would need Susan's help to complete the difficult problems she was assigning. Thus, they felt if Susan released the problem sets sooner, there would be more time to address difficult problems during class or during office hours earlier in the week.

Finally, Nikki spent time asking the students to explain how the slides Susan used during class helped or hindered their learning. Because the students made a range of comments about PowerPoint, Nikki decided to ask the students to describe how Susan used slides in the class and then address the specific comments on the board about slides. This conversation revealed that many of the students were not really sure how all of the little pieces of the class fit together into the big picture and that they felt they needed a refresher on some aspects of basic chem (which they own, but don't do). This resulted in them asking for things like more problem sets, words on the slides, or an overview at the beginning of class.

Nikki's conversation with the students revealed three themes for the debriefing conversation with Susan—(a) the role of the textbook, (b) the level and timing of problem sets, and (c) the big/little picture of the course. During Nikki's meeting with Susan (SGID Conversation 3), Nikki explained the issues Susan's students expressed during the SGID and offered Susan a chance to give her interpretation of the issues posed by the students, and together they discussed options for midcourse corrections. Susan knew that most of the students were not reading the text, so she felt compelled to lecture on the material to be sure that she covered everything in the book. She also thought she gave them plenty of time to do the problem sets, but now sees that her placement of office hours and due dates could be more carefully designed to ensure students had time and access to her office hours to complete the challenging work. She was also surprised that they wanted more practice problems, because she knew they struggled to complete problems she was assigning, but realized they were probably wanting practice problems that helped build their basic chemistry skills.

Based on the SGID results, Susan made a few midsemester course corrections. First, she decided to add more context for the reading assignments, letting the students know that she expected them to know new terms introduced in the chapter and that they would be able to answer the basic set of questions at the end of the chapter. To support this, she integrated a short reading quiz that students took before coming to class each day. Next, she polled the students to find out the best times to hold office hours and used that information to create a new office hour schedule that accommodated all of her students and the new project timeline. She also made two changes to the problem sets—she added some problems that help develop basic chemistry skills and released the problem sets on Friday, the week before they were due, to allow students more time to do their work and to seek help from her during class and new office hours. Finally, she developed a new concept map assignment that students worked on, collaboratively, to organize the content that Susan used in the review sessions for the exams.

SGID Sample Results—Nikki/Advanced Spanish Seminar

Nikki is a visiting assistant professor in the Spanish Department and teaches an upper division seminar course focused on current political issues in Spain. The enrollment in this course is 18 students who are either Spanish majors or minors. As described previously, Susan, one of Nikki's colleagues from the Chemistry Department, agreed to be the SGID consultant for her course. As was the case when Nikki did the SGID in Susan's class, the conversation that Susan had with Nikki's students gave Nikki some insights into her course that informed some midcourse corrections while also opening up a dialogue with the students about some critical aspects of the course. A cursory look at the feedback Nikki's students put up on the board suggested that Nikki helped learning by assigning great readings, adding her perspectives to the class and supporting rich discussions. However, the items in the hindering learning column suggested there were some trust issues between students, a lack of context for discussions, and some anxiety about the pressure to speak during class and saying the wrong thing. Finally, the students suggested learning could be improved in the class by having more clarity on due dates, reading quizzes, and other assignments, like the final project (see Table 3.2).

Susan started the conversation with Nikki's students by asking them to talk about the ways that class discussions helped and hindered their learning. This prompt allowed students to express that sometimes, due in part to their personal identities, they felt uncomfortable speaking about class topics. Their limited knowledge of the current culture in Spain and relevant historical facts that Nikki expected them to know also played into their reluctance to say more or offer their perspectives. This conversation led to some comments on the minute papers that Nikki asked students to complete at the end of each class. The students were not sure that the minute papers were

TABLE 3.2
SGID—Sample Results 2

Nikki—Spanish 378		
What Helps Your Learning in This Course?	*What Hinders Your Learning in This Course?*	*What Suggestions Do You Have to Improve Your Learning in This Class?*
• readings are great (+videos) • professor's additions/perspectives help and provocative questions • class discussions—we come in with an open mind • having people push back • fluidity of discussions • eye-opening discussions	• explanations of projects are confusing • pressure to speak in class for the minute papers—participation grades • lack of trust between students • worried about saying the wrong thing • not giving students lots of context/background content • minute papers • time management of projects	• logistics—concrete due dates and check-ins • restructure reading quizzes: takeaways, questions we had in lieu of specific questions • change minute papers • more warning or explanations for assignments • solidify assignment due dates

achieving the desired outcome—which they thought was an opportunity for reflection on what they talked about during class. Instead, many students expressed that knowing they must complete the minute papers at the end of class was a distraction during discussions. Rather than listening to the discussion, they found themselves trying to think about what they will be writing in the minute paper instead of fully participating in the discussion. They were also concerned that the reading quizzes were not targeted at the aspects of the reading that supported class discussions and distracted them from really reading the material and preparing for the discussions. Some students also told Susan that they simply looked for the answers to the reading quizzes instead of completing the reading. Finally, Susan talked with Nikki's students about the kind of clarity missing about assignments and due dates. For this part of the SGID, the students revealed that Nikki made numerous changes to the course calendar but they didn't know where to find the most recent information. Sometimes there was information on the course management site and other times Nikki emailed them changes to due dates. They also expressed that the information Nikki gave them about assignments like their final project was vague and they didn't really know what she wanted or how to get started on the project that included a blog post, video, and paper.

Susan's conversation with the students revealed three themes for the debriefing conversation with Nikki—(a) class discussions, (b) minute papers and reading quizzes, and (c) clarity on due dates and assignment expectations, especially the final project. During Susan's meeting with Nikki (SGID Conversation 3), Susan explained the issues Nikki's students expressed during the SGID and offered Nikki a chance to give her interpretation of the issues posed by the students, and together they discussed options for midcourse corrections. Nikki was a bit surprised to find out that her students were using the reading quiz as a way of preparing for class discussions. She had hoped that the reading quizzes would signal what details were important to know for class, but that they should also be fully completing the assigned readings that she thought were directly aligned with the learning outcomes for that week. The SGID results confirmed for Nikki what she had suspected, that some students were intimidated by class discussions given that many of their discussions asked students to talk, in Spanish, about contentious political issues in Spain such as gay marriage and abortion. Finally, Susan explained to Nikki that her students were having difficulty adjusting to schedule changes and were often confused about assignment expectations. Nikki was not aware that the students were struggling with due dates and expectations and had not received this feedback before from other students.

Informed by the SGID conversations, especially the post-SGID debrief with the students where she empathized with the students about the challenges posed by class discussions, Nikki and her students made the following midsemester course corrections. First, the students agreed to listen more intently during class discussions and to help Nikki create a space where they could constructively examine course topics, not their language skills. To help students feel more comfortable talking about contentious topics, Nikki assigned students roles and asked them to discuss the topics from this vantage point, instead of their own. She also had students work in teams at the beginning of each discussion class, to share ideas and provide each other feedback on their assigned roles and responses. She also changed the reading quizzes to allow students to not only answer a few, detailed questions but to also write more reflective answers to the discussion questions they would be exploring in class. Finally, after discussing the SGID feedback with her students, she decided to send a single, weekly communication that outlined the expectations for each week.

Instructor-to-Instructor SGIDs

Instructor-to-instructor SGIDs are in every way, shape, and form an SGID—a formative feedback experience that stimulates in-depth conversations with students, instructors, and SGID consultants. The learning environment of the course is enhanced through each conversation and by the careful reflection on the results that lead to purposeful midsemester course corrections. SGIDs make good courses better by revealing more than traditional surveys. Often the SGID experience addresses the disconnect in communication that grows between students and their instructors after the first day of class when the instructor reviewed the syllabus and other details of the course. More importantly, the SGID shrinks the gap between the student and faculty perceptions of a course, allowing students to examine the value of the work they are doing and offer insights from their perspectives on the ways the learning experience could be improved.

4

SGID PROGRAMS

My main exposure to an SGID program was probably a little different than it will be for most of our readers. At conferences I had heard whispers about it—a mention here or there—but I hadn't heard enough to get the full picture. Then, during the 2018/2019 school year I did a fellowship during my research sabbatical in the Center for Teaching and Learning at Colby College, and I got the chance to dig in deep. I got to have lots of conversations about the process with other consultants (mostly faculty), I had shadowing sessions, and I got to conduct dozens of SGIDs with instructors there. That was it for me; I was hooked.

I had the opportunity to learn about SGIDs and SGID programs in person, a luxury that many others will not have. But we hope that in this chapter and in those that follow, you will also find out what you need to know to start your own SGID programs.

After my fellowship ended, I returned to the University of the South and the position I held at the time as codirector of their Center for Teaching, and I got to work. I wanted to take all that I had learned and all the value I saw in SGID programs and situate them in the educational development context on my campus. Let me share some considerations that I made, which are likely also relevant to most CTLs when figuring out how to implement an SGID program.

The institution where I worked, the University of the South, is a liberal arts college, and at the time their Center for Teaching had two full-time faculty members who served as its codirectors. When I was codirector, we also had a volunteer advisory board of six faculty and staff members. We offer a suite of programming that is typical of other CTLs (e.g., a course design institute, an open-doors teaching week, faculty showcase presentations, faculty learning communities), but our staff, if you could call it that, was small. We communicated regularly with our faculty through a weekly email of events, and we enjoyed a good reputation as a welcoming and effective place for our faculty to discuss teaching.

Given this backdrop, it seemed smart to be measured in how we would integrate an SGID program into our work. As a relatively major program with no credibility on our campus yet, I decided to open it up broadly and to be clear about its function. With the goal of getting the word out, I decided not to directly integrate the SGID program into our portfolio of Center for Teaching programs—I wanted anyone and everyone who wanted in on the action to have their chance. I provided "teaser" messages about the program shortly before the school year started; then early in the semester I constructed an in-depth sign-up form. Because many faculty are a bit anxious about tenure and promotion processes, I made it explicitly clear that the SGID program would be completely confidential and would never be used to inform promotion and tenure decisions.

With the University of the South having a small center, I was also mindful of what it would take to have an SGID program grow in a manageable way. When I returned from my fellowship at Colby College, I quickly took up the task of training my other codirector on the process through some shadowing experiences, and the next semester we trained a handful of our advisory board members. But with those being trained and doing the training already filling roles as full-time faculty members, we had to start small, with each of us conducting between one and five SGIDs a semester.

Determining how we would help develop our instructors was also on our minds as we got the program off the ground. Our newer faculty, some of whom had very little teaching experience, came in droves. We were happy to have the SGID process be a major way in which they got to know both good pedagogy and the services of our center. But we were also explicit about recruiting more veteran faculty as well. Although many of them felt confident in their teaching, we reached out to some of our longtime "frequent flyers," and they were excited to try a new way to get feedback. We also hoped that they would spread the word that SGIDs aren't just for our newest faculty.

We also made sure to assess our work and gather quantitative and qualitative feedback about how valuable our faculty found the program to be (we were thrilled the feedback was so positive!). We used this feedback to bolster our new SGID program's credibility to the administration, and to impel first-time faculty members to give it a try.

Although when we started the program we were not as direct about gathering assessment feedback from students, it came through anyway in anecdotal reports. We heard—either during the SGID sessions or after the in-class session had wrapped—comments like "I'm really glad we have a chance to talk about this as a class," "This helped me think differently about why we do the readings in here," or, maybe as a bit of a sly insinuation, "This class is going great, but could you do this in my next class?" All of this information let me know we were definitely on the right track for a new program that would help faculty make meaningful alterations to their courses.

—Jordan D. Troisi

Once a few instructors start using the SGID to collect midcourse feedback, word spreads and more instructors want some of this pedagogical magic. Whether you are an instructor who started to do SGIDs with other instructors, the chair of the faculty development committee, or an educational developer, starting an SGID program might be the next item on your programming list. This chapter outlines how to start a thriving SGID program that brings SGID magic to more instructors across your institution. We provide advice from our experiences starting SGID programs along with a range of ideas to support a thriving and sustainable SGID program. We offer pragmatic advice gleaned from our combined experiences starting and sustaining SGID programs at our institutions. Our advice ranges from the *Gosh, that would have been nice to know sooner* to *Who knew that would happen?* kinds of insights. Mostly, we unpack our heads for you in this chapter, revealing our true geekiness, because in the end, it pays to attend to the large and small details of a program like the SGID.

SGID Program Basics and Logistics

If you have made it to this part of the book, you are probably getting excited about starting an SGID program at your institution. And although it seems really simple to send out an email to your instructors, saying come one, come all to the greatest faculty development show on Earth, you might want to pause to consider a few programming details that we think will help you launch a successful program. We review the basics, logistics, and rollout options for launching an SGID program at your institution (Figure 4.1). Later, in chapter 7 we delve into ways to enhance SGIDs and SGID programs, including strategies to expand the reach of the SGID program, improve consultant training, and create productive dialogues about the SGID. But first we will focus on establishing an SGID program that is valued and respected by students, instructors, and the administration.

To get started, you should consider the *SGID program basics*—what to call your SGID program, when to offer SGIDs (defining *midsemester*), which set of questions to use during the in-class SGID session to collect student feedback (Table 1.4), and who will serve as your inaugural team of SGID consultants. Additionally, there are a handful of *SGID program logistics* you will need to consider to ensure your SGID program runs smoothly. These logistical items include the registration and scheduling methods you will use to collect information from instructors, communications to connect SGID consultants to instructors, how many SGIDs you have the capacity to offer, how to protect instructor and student confidentiality, and the methods to

Figure 4.1. Elements for SGID program development.

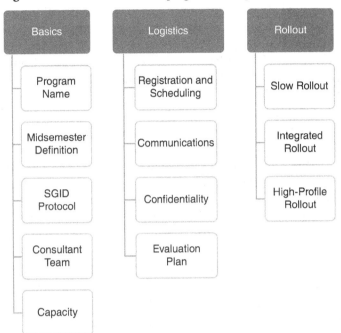

evaluate the quality and impact of the program. Finally, we consider three rollout plans to introduce the SGID to your campus—the slow rollout plan, the integrated rollout plan, and the high-profile rollout plan. There is not much literature that informs this section of the book. Instead the three of us will do our best to integrate our own experiences along with ideas and advice we have obtained from colleagues at other institutions about their SGID programs.

Program Name

One of the most important decisions you need to make about your SGID program is what to call it. This may seem like an odd way to start this chapter, given that we have spent the entire book calling the SGID the SGID. But truth be told, although the name *small group instructional diagnosis* is meant to be descriptive, it doesn't really help instructors and administrators understand who is working in small groups, what aspects of instruction are being diagnosed, and who is performing the diagnosis. Not to mention that *diagnosis* certainly makes it sound like a problem or two exists in the course already. It is unlikely that any name for the SGID would succeed at fully describing the process, but some names are better at demystifying both the process and the intended impact. The names we use are "Mid-Semester Course Analysis" (MSCA, Colby College), "Mid-Semester Group Analysis" (MSGA, University of the South), and "Mid-Semester Interview About Teaching" (MIT, Grand Valley State University). Other naming options that attempt to make the SGID more welcoming include "Group Instructional Feedback Technique" (GIFT), "Student Perceptions Of Instruction" (SPOI), or "Interim Course Feedback" (ICM). Additional names for the SGID emphasize the process (Structured Focus Groups, Midterm Chat) or the questions (Bare Bones Questions, Keep Doing-Quit Doing-Start Doing). Other names embrace the teaching focus of the SGID (Teaching Analysis Poll, Teaching Analysis by Students). We compiled a list of alternative SGID names from the literature (Holton et al., 2016) and gleaned from survey responses from other CTL directors and staff. Feel free to use any of these names or come up with your own name for the SGID (Holton et al., 2016; see Table 4.1). Once you have the name for your SGID program, start using it as much as possible and before you know it, other people will be using the name and then you will know that your SGID program is a real thing.

TABLE 4.1
Alternative Names for the SGID

Includes *Midsemester, Midterm,* or *Midcourse*
- Midcourse Evaluation (ME)
- Midcourse Formative reviews (MFR)
- Midsemester Assessment (MSA)
- Midsemester Class Check-in (MSCC)
- Midsemester Course Analysis (MSCA)
- Midsemester Formative Evaluation (MSFE)
- Midsemester Focus Groups (MSFG)
- Midsemester Group Analysis (MSGA)
- Midsemester Interview about Teaching (MIT)
- Midterm Assessment Process (MAP)
- Midterm Assessments of Teaching (MAT)
- Midterm Chat (MC)
- Midterm Feedback (MF)
- Midterm Instructional Diagnosis (MID)
- Midterm Student Feedback (MSF)
- Standardized Midterm Evaluations (SME)

Includes *Teaching* or *Instruction*
- Formative Assessment of Classroom Teaching (FACT)
- Group Instructional Feedback Technique (GIFT)
- Instructional Diagnosis (ID)
- Midterm Instructional Diagnosis (MID)
- Students Consulting On Teaching (SCOT)
- Student Perception Of Instruction (SPOI)
- Teaching Analysis Poll (TAP)
- Teaching Analysis by Students (TABS)

Descriptive Names
- Bare Bone Questions (BBQ)
- Classroom Learning Interview Process (CLIP)
- Early Course Feedback Focus Groups (ECFFG)
- Engaging Students' Perspectives (ESP)
- Keep doing, Quit doing, Start doing (KQS)
- Quick Course Diagnosis (QCD)
- Small Group Perception (SGP)
- Structured Focus Groups (SGF)
- Student Feedback through Consensus (SFC)
- Student Group Analysis (SGA)
- Two Survey Method (TSM)

Midsemester Definition

One of the cornerstones of the SGID experience is that instructors receive actionable feedback they can use to implement midcourse corrections. Thus, the SGID experience is best positioned during the middle of the semester, which begs the question—when does the midsemester timeframe start and end? Answering this question is harder than it seems because you want to start offering SGIDs after students have had some significant, graded learning experience and before it is too late in the term for the instructor to make use of the SGID feedback. Thus, determining what *midsemester* means for your campus is an important first step in setting up an SGID program. If you try to start the SGIDs too soon in the term, students really haven't had enough experience in the course to offer meaningful feedback that would inform any midcourse corrections by the instructor (Snooks et al., 2004). Defining the midsemester block as the 1 or 2 weeks square in the middle of your term limits the number of SGIDs that can be reasonably accomplished. Thus, to accommodate more SGIDs and be mindful of consultant and instructor schedules, the midsemester block for SGIDs should include

TABLE 4.2
Midsemester Blocks and SGID Scheduling

Academic Calendar	Start Midsemester Block	End Midsemester Block
15/16-week semester	Week 5/6	Week 10/11
12/13-week trimester	Week 4/5	Week 8/9
10-week quarter	Week 3/4	Week 6/7

4–5 weeks, depending on the length of the term. We offer midsemester block options for academic calendars based on semesters, trimesters, and quarters (Table 4.2). For each type of academic calendar, we placed the start of the midsemester block late enough in the term to ensure that students in most courses have completed, and received feedback on, a major, graded assignment or exam. The end of the midsemester block allows faculty who elect a later SGID schedule to make use of the feedback to inform course corrections for that group of students. Each of these options spreads the SGID program across a number of weeks that may or may not include a break, which is also important to factor into your planning. It is worth noting that you will need to develop modified timelines for SGIDs offered for shorter terms or block courses that have a different definition of *midsemester*. Managing SGIDs for these kinds of courses and situations can easily be accomplished by offering a special opportunity during the SGID registration process to collect the necessary details.

SGID Protocol

Next you should develop the SGID protocol for your program. Thus, you should consider whether your SGID program will include either of the optional SGID elements described in chapter 1—the SGID premeeting between instructor and consultant to discuss the course and an in-class observation prior to engaging the students in SGID Conversations 1 and 2. You should also consider which set of questions from chapter 1 you will use to seed the SGID conversations of your program. If you are starting a new program, you may want to start with one of the three-question sets, to ensure you make the most use of the 30-minute in-class time block. However, you may opt for a question set that aligns with your campus culture or other priorities. Alternatively, you may want to ask colleagues across academic disciplines to indicate which questions they find most compelling and use that information to determine the best set of questions for your institutional context. We find it useful to select a set of questions and use them across all

SGIDs and only make changes, if necessary, between academic years. And of course, you will need to clearly explain each element of your SGID program to the instructors, because they will not be familiar with this kind of program and we have run into issues with faculty who don't know what to do when the SGID consultant arrives in the classroom or don't understand that the SGID consultation occurs during class time.

Finally, you should decide on the kind of report SGID consultants will produce after their work with the students to provide to the instructor during SGID Conversation 3. Many centers utilize reports that only contain the SGID feedback that the students put up on the board. Others develop more nuanced reports that include notes from the in-class observations, if applicable, the SGID results students put on the board, and the consultant's summary of these notes. From our experience, many instructors submit SGID reports in their annual reports or other dossiers, so it is worth considering the kinds of information you want reviewed by department and university evaluation groups. We offer a few sample SGID reports for your consideration in Appendix A.

> **Sidebar:** Many instructors feel that it would be difficult to "lose" 30 minutes of class time and engage in an SGID. Ironically in this circumstance, the SGID requires a greater time commitment on the part of the consultant than either the instructor or students. On our campus, consultants are also faculty. Nevertheless, it proves to be an ongoing conundrum how best to respond to instructors who feel that class time is too precious to give over to this folly. Our most compelling arguments have not come from our center but close colleagues who have engaged in an SGID previously and can speak directly to the benefits. The instructors who have participated in SGIDs through our center more often than not become more engaged in other center programs, whether through additional consultation, faculty learning communities, or workshops. It would be an interesting research project, actually, to investigate the differences among instructors who readily give class time over to an SGID as compared to those who stoutly refuse and insist that their content delivery takes precedence.—Christine M. Rener

Consultant Team

Another basic element of starting an SGID program is building a team of SGID consultants. The best place to start when growing your SGID consultant team is with the members of the CTL. However, if the staffing of the CTL is small, then consider inviting instructors who are respected by the campus community for their teaching and leadership. We think the best SGID consultants are thoughtful educational developers or instructors who are interested in the role of student feedback in making midcourse corrections. The SGID consultants do not need to be expert instructors, but should have some undergraduate teaching experience, which helps inform the work with students and instructors. It is also desirable, but not essential, that SGID consultants have experienced the SGID in one of their courses, not only so they understand the process but so they can empathize with the instructors who may have some anxiety around having their students engage in this kind of feedback experience.

Now that you will be offering the SGID to a wider audience of instructors, training consultants to align with the tenets of your SGID program is essential to establish program quality, ensure consistent messaging about the SGID, create a safe and welcoming experience for students, and provide a confidential and formative consultation experience with the instructors about the SGID results. And although we think that consultants should receive iterative training experiences to improve their skills as SGID consultants, the initial consultant training does not need to be overly exhaustive. We present a more in-depth perspective of consultant training in chapter 7. But for the purposes of getting an SGID program up and running, consultants should have had an SGID in their course, watched a trained consultant run an SGID (in-class conversation and faculty consultation), been observed doing the in-class SGID and follow-up faculty consultation, and provided with feedback on their facilitation skills. Additionally, SGID consultants should receive a consultant manual that includes all of the necessary logistics, form templates, sample email communications, processes, and details. We provide a sample consultant manual from the SGID programs at Grand Valley State University that includes lots of additional details to supplement the information provided in chapter 1 (see Appendix B).

Sidebar: Particularly as we were getting our SGID program off the ground, it was helpful to review draft instructor reports with other center staff serving as SGID consultants, just to get a sense of whether or not we were on the right track with our debrief conversation plans. Now that our program has matured, we still find value (and a great deal of excitement) in checking in—sharing interesting themes or general trends in issues that students raise, cool new pedagogical strategies that instructors are using, and so on.—Christine M. Rener

Capacity

The issue of SGID capacity is an important consideration when starting an SGID program. If you are a center of one, you can only reasonably engage in a limited number of SGIDs per week, given your other time commitments. If you are part of a larger center, members of your staff or instructors you have recruited to support the SGID program will also have time constraints that impact how many SGIDs they can manage per term. Thus, it is useful to envision a modest number of SGIDs that your center can conduct per week to reflect the lived realities of your team. As we explored in chapter 1, the SGID, from setting up the SGID to completing the faculty consultation, takes about 4 hours of work, or more if your SGID process includes a longer classroom observation component or other variations (Black, 1998). Thus, you should expect each SGID to consume about 5 hours of consultant time, when you factor in email communications and preparation time. Determining your SGID capacity helps ensure that you offer quality SGID experiences to instructors and is crucial in determining how to market the SGID consultations to solicit requests that align with your center's SGID capacity. Starting small by offering a modest number of SGIDs allows you to get the process right, ensuring that instructors have a positive experience.

Registration and Scheduling

The next phase of SGID program development is the event planning component of this chapter. Depending on how much experience you have running other programs, you may want to skip over this part of the chapter. However, given the complexity of the SGID program, we are hopeful that the advice we offer will help both novice and expert event planners. Successfully running an SGID program requires a robust marketing and registration process along with strategies to schedule SGIDs that effectively connect consultants to the instructors they will be working with. Additionally, the SGID program should include processes to ensure instructor and student confidentiality and a plan to evaluate the quality and impact of the program.

SGID marketing should align with strategies you utilize to advertise other programs and services, with special attention to select audiences that you think would benefit from an SGID experience, such as new faculty and faculty who have recently designed or redesigned one of their courses. Once the concept of the SGID takes hold, you can integrate SGID marketing into the methods you use to market other programs—emails, newsletters, center website, and word of mouth. In our marketing and informal conversations, we encourage faculty who have had an SGID in previous terms or semesters to engage in the SGID on a regular basis. Even if the feedback provided to the instructor during each SGID highlights similar issues, the value of engaging the students in the SGID certainly is worth the time investment. We also encourage department chairs and other administrators to champion the SGID experience to their faculty. But we discourage administrators from requiring instructors to have an SGID or suggesting that SGID results should be included in annual reports or other evaluation dossiers required for promotion or tenure procedures. Both of these decisions, to get an SGID and how to use the SGID results, are decisions that instructors should make voluntarily.

There are two ways to approach SGID program registration and scheduling—rolling and advanced request. From the instructor's perspective both of these systems look very similar—the CTL puts out a call for SGID requests with deadlines for submitting the requests. In the rolling system, the CTL schedules each SGID as they are received. However, the advanced request system waits until all the requests are submitted to build the SGID schedule for the term. Regardless of which process you select, it is helpful to develop an SGID request form that collects all of the information you will need to schedule and conduct SGIDs. The form should collect details about the instructor (e.g., name, department, pronouns, academic rank), course (e.g., number, name, class schedule, location, number of students), and preferred dates for the SGID (first and second choices). We provide marketing text and a sample registration form in Appendix C. Soliciting SGID voluntary requests from faculty and instructors, including teaching postdoctoral fellows and graduate students, can be accomplished using this form. Also, if you have a team of SGID consultants, you want to consider the following situational factors when making the assignments: consultant schedule, consultant capacity, disciplinary homes of the instructor and consultant, and experience of the consultant. We attempt to schedule consultants to SGIDs outside of their departments and colleges, if possible. We also avoid assigning SGIDs in large classes or using alternative formats to new SGID consultants. If you opt for the advanced request registration process, you can also ensure that instructors who request more than one SGID are matched with the same SGID consultant, which often saves time because the consultant and instructor can meet once to debrief all of the requested SGIDs.

The rolling registration process typically starts a week or two before the midsemester start date on your campus. Using the communication process established by your center or institution, inform instructors that you are accepting rolling SGID requests until capacity is reached. In this process, the SGID schedule is built one SGID request at a time. Upon receipt of the SGID request, select details (class time, preferred date for SGID, and number of students) for each SGID are sent to the SGID consultant team. Again, to promote a culture of confidentiality, all of the consultants do not need to know which instructors are requesting an SGID, because the CTL has all of the requested information and will make appropriate assignments based on instructor discipline and consultant experience and capacity. Consultants who are available for the requested SGIDs respond to the CTL, which assigns the SGID to the consultant who is the best fit from those who indicated their availability for the SGID class time. The CTL then connects the consultant with the instructor to engage in the SGID with the students and instructor (see the next section for more on the communication process).

The rolling registration process requires less advanced planning on the part of the instructor, allowing them to request SGIDs over a multiweek block. This process also allows the SGID scheduling to be more flexible and responsive to the changing nature of instructor and consultant schedules. This registration and scheduling system allows the CTL to select the most appropriate consultant, limited only by the consultants who respond to each SGID request. Thus, the rolling registration process often includes multiple email communications, including additional emails to both instructors and the full consultant team if the CTL is unable to find a consultant for a particular SGID and has to solicit additional scheduling options. The process may also underutilize consultants who would have wanted to do more SGIDs but didn't respond in a timely manner or had scheduling conflicts pop up as the semester progressed. Additionally, the rolling process may require ongoing marketing efforts to solicit participation and keep the program viable throughout the entire midsemester course block. Deploying additional marketing increases the workload for the CTL and can often turn instructors off to the SGID.

The advanced request method of SGID registration and scheduling uses the same SGID request form, but instead of opening the registration window for multiple weeks, the CTL sets an SGID request deadline early in the term, typically at the end of the 1st or 2nd week of classes. This early registration deadline allows the CTL to prioritize marketing about the SGID early in the term, while faculty are finalizing their course schedules. The common deadline allows the CTL to collect *all* of the SGID requests and build the SGID schedule for the entire term. To build the schedule, the program manager shares select SGID details with the consultant team (e.g., class time, preferred date for SGID, and number of students), determines their availability for each SGID request, and asks each consultant to provide their SGID capacity for the term. This method also allows the CTL to intentionally match consultants with instructors outside of their department or area and assign the same consultant to instructors who request multiple SGIDs, which limits consultation scheduling and time.

The advanced request process allows instructors and consultants to plan in advance for the SGID, allowing instructors to build it into their syllabi and for consultants to manage the number of SGIDs they take on per week or term. The other advantage of this method is that it creates energy at the beginning of the term about the SGID, resulting in more interest in the SGID and, often, more requests. The preregistration method does not solve the problem of matching consultants to the requested SGID times and dates; this part will be a bit complicated no matter what. However, it does allow the CTL to connect with instructors early in the term to resolve scheduling conflicts. The other con of this method is that sometimes (read as almost always) some instructors miss the deadline and request an SGID after the full schedule has been developed and disseminated. This situation is easily remedied by asking consultants who have additional capacity to consider the additional request or to communicate to the instructor that their request cannot be filled at such a late date and encourage them to submit their request earlier next term.

Communications

Connecting the SGID consultant with the instructor is the last phase of the registration process and is independent of the process used to collect and assign the SGIDs to the consultants. During this communication, the CTL connects the consultant with the instructor and includes all course and instructor details. The message also indicates the assigned date, location, consultant arrival time, and the start and end time of the in-class portion of the SGID (Appendix D). The message asks the instructor to reach out to the consultant to schedule the post-SGID planning meeting (SGID Conversation 3) and to provide the consultant with relevant course materials (e.g., syllabus, assignment prompts) and other pertinent details, such as confirming the classroom location, the kind of writing surface in the classroom, whether students are used to working in groups, and other facets of the course they want to share with the consultant. The CTL should also encourage the consultants to reach out to the instructors if they don't hear back from the instructor within a day or two. After the CTL connects the consultant with the instructor, the consultant sets up the post-SGID meeting, sends the CTL an electronic version of the SGID report, and alerts the CTL regarding any issues or problems, especially if the SGID had to be rescheduled or canceled for any reason. Sample text for these communications are also found in Appendix D.

Confidentiality

Unlike workshops or other educational development programs, the SGID program requires a heightened attention to confidentiality given the detailed information provided by the students to the consultant about the instructor and course. And although we believe that the SGID should not be viewed as evaluative or as an indication that the instructor is experiencing difficulties with their courses, we know the SGID process and results may be misinterpreted. To ensure the confidentiality of process and results, the CTL should limit the distribution of instructor names and other identifying information to administrators or faculty and only release detailed information to the SGID consultants for their assigned sessions. The consultant should be instructed to limit the amount of time they wait outside of the classroom prior to the SGID. If they are asked by a passing administrator or instructor about their visit to a classroom, the consultant should simply indicate the visit was requested by the instructor for instructional purposes or indicate they are working with this instructor on a project. As mentioned in chapters 1 and 3, SGID consultants should discuss the confidentiality of the SGID process and results with the students, explain that their instructor requested this service, and indicate that the results obtained from the SGID will only be given to the instructor to inform any mid- or postcourse corrections that seem appropriate. The consultant should also let the students know that they will keep student identities confidential when debriefing with the instructor to ensure that the professor doesn't align any of the SGID feedback with certain students. This is particularly important if the consultant knows any of the students from other courses or activities. SGID consultants should shred the paper copies of the student feedback forms used during the in-class portion of the SGID. Additionally, any electronic copies of SGID results should only be sent to the instructor or CTL, where they may be used for evaluation or potential research purposes and maintained on secured computers or servers. Finally, members of the CTL or SGID team should not share, even in passing conversations, the names of instructors who participated in the SGID program, unless you have the permission of the instructor.

Evaluation Plan

The last item to consider related to SGID logistics is program evaluation. Developing an evaluation strategy for your SGID can be as simple or as complex as you like, depending on what you are trying to measure and the goals of your SGID program. We dive deeper into this topic in chapter 8, but in the early stages of an SGID program you can survey faculty on their experience with the SGID. Many studies demonstrate that students and faculty prefer the SGID to other methods of collecting student feedback (Abbott et al., 1990; Heppner & Johnston, 1994; Mauger, 2010). You may want to confirm this for your context, but you may also want to determine what students and instructors at your institution think about the SGID by collecting feedback about their satisfaction with the SGID, using the items and methods described by others (Abbott et al., 1990; Heppner & Johnston, 1994; Mauger, 2010). We have included some sample evaluations items we use to collect information on the quality of the consultation with the SGID consultant and the impact of the SGID experience on the instructor's learning about select aspects of teaching (Table 4.3).

TABLE 4.3
Sample SGID Program Evaluation Items

Evaluation Items	Purpose
During the SGID • I was exposed to evidence-based content. • I was exposed to actionable ideas. • I exchanged ideas with faculty from other disciplines. • I felt comfortable. • I experienced a supportive environment. • I interacted with a consultant who demonstrated a positive demeanor. • I felt my situation was understood. • I felt my needs were met.	Evaluate quality and impact of consultation with instructor.
As a result of the SGID, I made progress toward • developing relationships that enhance teaching. • expanding my pedagogical appreciation. • incorporating feedback to inform teaching. • designing courses that stimulate learning. • integrating knowledge about how learning works to enhance learning. • deepening diversity through my teaching. • deepening inclusivity through my teaching.	Analyze impact on faculty learning about elements of teaching.

SGID Program Rollout Plans

Jordan's story at the start of this chapter explores one way to start an SGID program—carefully build it, train a group of instructors, and then open it up to all faculty. We call this the high-profile rollout plan. The success that the SGID program at the University of the South experienced was based, in part, on Jordan's careful planning, experience doing SGIDs at Colby College, and the welcoming and inclusive messaging he used to invite faculty to this programming opportunity. What are the other secrets to SGID program success? How can you effectively market this program to faculty and administrators in a way that lives up to what the SGID is and what the SGID is not? When we asked educational developers who do not offer SGIDs at their institutions ($n = 84$) the reasons they do not offer this program, the two most common responses were insufficient personnel and uncertainty regarding faculty buy-in. We will explore ways to address personnel issues in chapter 7 but do want to spend some time considering the issue of faculty buy-in, because we feel that getting faculty buy-in is absolutely essential for any educational development program, especially the SGID.

Getting buy-in from faculty and administrators should precede widespread marketing efforts or full implementation of the SGID program. The teaching climate at most institutions supports an individualistic approach to teaching, often touted as part of the academic freedom that faculty have to develop and teach courses without excessive, or any, oversight (Chavez & Longerbeam, 2016). This kind of teaching culture often is wary of the role of peer observations of teaching and typically uses observations for summative evaluation experiences, supporting tenure and promotion processes. However, some institutions support a formative approach to teaching evaluations, where instructors are encouraged to seek out feedback, at many points during the semester, from students and colleagues. Introducing the SGID to a group of faculty enculturated in an individualist approach to teaching might meet resistance, whereas faculty from institutions that support a formative approach to teaching may welcome the SGID experience. Of course, there may be faculty at both types of institutions who are threatened by the idea of the SGID process and may need to learn about this program using strategies besides email and web-based communications. Ultimately, getting faculty buy-in involves communicating the value of the SGID as a tool to inform midcourse corrections, addressing the time commitment involved in the SGID process, and situating the SGID within the other institutional constructs used to collect and provide feedback on teaching (e.g., end-of-semester evaluations, peer evaluations). These concerns about starting and sustaining an SGID program can be managed by an effective rollout plan. We provide three approaches to start an SGID program at your institution—(a) slow rollout, (b) integrated rollout, and (c) high-profile rollout.

Slow Rollout Plan

The slow rollout plan leverages faculty interest in collecting and using student feedback about teaching. This plan starts by offering a few programs at the beginning of the term on midsemester feedback, more broadly, with a focus on the best practices to inform midcourse corrections. Additional programs in this preliminary phase could include programs on ways to respond to end-of-semester student evaluations. Both of these programming venues would include discussions about the ways that midsemester feedback often improves student ratings and results in more in-depth and constructive feedback. More importantly, these programs can introduce the SGID as one of the methods available to collect meaningful feedback from their students during the middle of the semester. The SGID can then be offered to the workshop participants as one way to implement ideas gleaned from these workshops. Once these participants have had the opportunity to use the SGID in one or more of their courses, the next phase of the slow rollout plan lets the SGID sell itself. This group of instructors, given their interest in using student feedback to inform their teaching, will undoubtedly learn something new about their courses from the SGID. Invite this group of instructors to cofacilitate workshops or roundtable discussions about midsemester feedback with another group of instructors. Continue this programming cycle until you build a strong group of SGID supporters, who may also be invited to join the consultant team. Once there is enough support from the instructors and you have built a consultant team, offer the SGID to select departments or programs, or if you have the capacity, to all instructors.

Integrated Rollout Plan

The integrated rollout plan also takes a slow approach to introducing the SGID to your colleagues, and does so by integrating the SGID experience within established programs, such as faculty learning communities, new faculty programming, or mentoring experiences. Integrating the SGID into programs where faculty are working together on topics or processes that support their work provides a safe place for conversations and informal experiences with the SGID. In this setting, faculty engage in the SGID in teams of two or three, either engaging one another or a trained consultant to conduct the SGID. Thus, integrating the SGID into other programs empowers faculty to experience the

SGID as instructor *and* consultant, using the results to inform their teaching and the work of the cohort (e.g., integrating active learning into teaching, providing context for mentoring conversations). Seeing the SGID from both views offers instructors a more comprehensive view of the SGID, one that they will likely share with other colleagues. And although confidentiality of the SGID is still important when the SGID is being used more informally, by a group of faculty, establishing ground rules related to confidentiality is often part of learning communities and other cohort-based programs. Integrating the SGID into other programs expands the reach of the SGID to other groups of faculty who did not attend other workshops or roundtable discussions.

High-Profile Rollout Plan

Finally, we end this chapter where we started, with Jordan's example of a high-profile rollout. High-profile rollouts of the SGID rely on strong, reciprocal relationships between the CTL and the faculty. When the center has a strong reputation for quality programming, adding the SGID to the portfolio of programs will likely be viewed positively by the administration and faculty. To ensure successful implementation of an SGID program, the CTL should engage stakeholders, such as department chairs and promotion committees, in discussions about the SGID. Prior to opening SGID registration, the CTL should develop comprehensive resources, relevant literature (including our book), and communications to educate the academic community about the promise of the SGID and the ways this experience will inform course corrections and many other aspects of the teaching and learning landscape. The CTL should also provide details on how the quality and impact of the SGID program will be evaluated.

Summary of SGID Program Elements

We have provided a lot of details about starting an SGID program: the basics, the logistics, and the rollout. But ultimately, there are a few key things that this chapter boils down to:

- *Context matters.* What your SGID program looks like depends a lot on your CTL and your institution.
- *Instructors matter.* Who your instructors are matters a great deal in how they will hear about and sign up for the SGID.
- *Selling the SGID (marketing) matters.* It's important to heed recommendations that make sense, in your context, that will help your SGID program start and thrive.

- *Planning matters.* Review the elements in Figure 4.1 and the appendices with your planning team, advisory group, or a small group of faculty. Talking through the considerations of program basics, logistics, and rollout plans with other people on our campuses has been instrumental in developing robust SGID programs.

PART THREE

MAKING THE CASE

5

THE IMPACT OF THE
SGID ON THE COURSE

Is the course sufficiently challenging?
Am I going too fast? Am I clear?
Has class time enabled them to practice and improve their skills?
Is there too much lecture? Is there enough?
What are their perspectives on breadth versus depth?
Are they following along with the learning objectives?
Are they receiving adequate feedback?
I am trying a new teaching style. How do they feel it is going compared to their typical courses?

These questions are just a sampling of what instructors have shared with me as reasons for requesting an SGID. At my university, we make it a practice of sending instructors an email requesting (a) confirmation of the SGID time and location, (b) confirmation of the follow-up consultation, (c) a copy of the syllabus, and (d) any special concerns or areas of focus for the SGID. Although not everyone provides a response to this last item, the critically reflective questions noted at the beginning are commonly cited reasons for requesting an SGID. If instructors have other ways of going about getting feedback from their students, what is special about the SGID? Why do colleagues recommend the SGID to one another? Why do departmental mentoring plans highly recommend the SGID for new faculty? Why do instructors ask for additional SGIDs when trying another new approach in a subsequent semester? Why does a student send me a note thanking me for coming to their class and conducting the SGID? For me, the answers to these questions are revealed most clearly during the post-SGID consultation with the instructor. Several years ago, an instructor in their second semester of teaching requested an SGID, citing concerns about a new approach to grading that was quite different from what students were experiencing in other courses in the department. The instructor was interested in student feedback about the grading scheme, wanting to ensure that it was perceived as clear and also fair. During the SGID, the grading scheme was not mentioned by any of the students and, in fact, the feedback was nearly universally complimentary of many other aspects of the course. Student comments included the following:

- *The professor cares about student success.*
- *The professor is approachable and flexible.*
- *The professor is passionate and inspiring.*
- *Case studies help us apply the information.*
- *Tests are fair.*
- *Slow down a touch on slides during lectures.*

During the consultant–student debrief of the student group feedback up on the whiteboard (SGID Conversation 2), I gently probed and asked for any comment about the grading. Students praised the clarity of the course syllabus, but otherwise didn't have anything else to say about grading practices. In reviewing the student feedback during the instructor consultation, the instructor was visibly touched by what the students had to say. We talked about how nervous they had been leading up to the SGID (as well as leading up to the follow-up consultation) and what a boost this feedback was during a difficult 1st year. That students noticed how much they cared and worked to help students learn was not at all what the instructor anticipated from having an SGID. Having kept in touch with this instructor, I have learned about the ways that they have strived to not only continue to refine their grading practices, but to also lean into a supportive learning environment and challenge their students to engage in increasingly complex team-based projects. This instructor has been recognized as an outstanding educator in their department, led workshops in other departments, and, not surprisingly, recommended the SGID to their colleagues along the way.

—Christine M. Rener

The SGID process itself is ostensibly about gathering feedback from students and, in the process, engaging instructors and students in rich conversations about teaching and learning and encouraging metacognitive reflection. What we (and others) have learned is that by scratching below the surface, the SGID has the potential to impact those involved in meaningful and long-lasting ways. In this chapter, we will take a detailed, evidence-based look at the SGID, exploring its impacts on a course, the students, and the instructor. We have gathered evidence from a number of sources: (a) research on the SGID itself; (b) studies using the

SGID as a research tool to probe instructional practices, learning environments, and the impact of curricular revisions; (c) our own experience as educational developers; and (d) the survey and interviews conducted for this book project. Themes that emerge from our analysis derive from multiple avenues of investigation and lend support to our assertion that the SGID is an extremely worthwhile endeavor. We will highlight the ways in which the SGID improves the learning environment. For students, the SGID has been demonstrated to impact perception of a course, perception of an instructor, engagement in learning-oriented behaviors, and motivation. For instructors, the SGID holds the promise of improving perception of a course, perception of students, a sense of belonging to an institution, and end-of-semester student feedback.

Making the Most of a Midsemester Opportunity

The SGID typically takes place near the middle of the semester, the ideal time to gather formative feedback about the course so that any changes or clarifications can be acted upon and improve the remainder of the course. Much can be said about the value of pausing at the midpoint of a course, taking stock of what has transpired thus far, considering the current moment, and turning one's gaze toward the time remaining. No matter the project, the middle can be a turning point with potential that can either be tapped or ignored (see, e.g., the treatment of midpoints by Daniel Pink, 2018, in his fourth chapter of *When: The Scientific Secrets of Perfect Timing*).

Collecting midsemester feedback itself is a practice with demonstrable impact on the learning environment and favorable student and instructor perceptions. Instructors who administer midsemester surveys are more likely to be perceived as committed to teaching, their students, and student success (Brown, 2008). Students report improvement in their own learning and an even stronger commitment to further study in the discipline (McDonnell & Dodd, 2017; McGowan, 2009; Overall & Marsh, 1979). Beyond perceptions, studies have shown higher end-of-semester student ratings and better student performance in courses for which instructors have administered a midsemester feedback survey or otherwise established measurable rapport with students (Lammers et al., 2017; McGowan, 2009). The same cannot be said for student and instructor perspectives of the utility of end-of-semester ratings (Brown, 2008; Wulff et al., 1985).

If a curious, reflective instructor chooses to gather midsemester feedback through an anonymous survey or even an instructor-facilitated class discussion, chances are high that the resulting feedback will not be particularly detailed or frank. The instructor will most often be left to interpret student comments in isolation. Taking the next step and engaging with a consultant to review the feedback has been shown to be an impactful practice. A meta-analysis by Peter Cohen (1980) showed improvement in end-of-semester ratings for instructors receiving midsemester feedback and a larger gain for those also engaging in a consultation. There is even some evidence that these improvements remain, even several years after the consultation session (Piccinin, 1999). So, consultations matter. And the most effective consultations are substantive in design, bringing multiple sources of information to bear on the discussion and engaging the instructor actively (e.g., collaboratively exploring feedback, working through ways to approach responding to students, etc.; Penny & Coe, 2004).

Putting the pieces together, we contend that the SGID capitalizes not only on the potential of the midsemester point in time, but also provides rich, detailed student feedback collected and synthesized in a meaningful way by a consultant external to the course. The SGID also builds on the impactful conversation with the consultant, actively engaging the instructor in considering and responding to the feedback. In an extraordinarily synergistic way, the SGID allows an instructor to combine the value of students as experts at assessing their own response to a class with the professional knowledge and experience of an educational developer or peer (Ackerman et al., 2009; Overall & Marsh, 1979).

What Do Students Actually Say?

Before we turn to the evidence supporting the effectiveness of the SGID, it might be helpful to pause here and consider what kinds of feedback result from the process. In short, what students have to say is substantive and important. As detailed in the following, evidence has accumulated along common themes of both student responses as well as descriptors of the favorable impacts of the SGID—as reported by students and instructors. Instructors are sometimes surprised that the relatively broad questions asked during the SGID can elicit such specific, actionable feedback. We believe that it is not a coincidence that students engage so deeply with the nondirective format of the SGID, a refreshing departure from the approach taken on most SETs and surveys wherein students rate their level of agreement with predetermined items. The richness and specificity of the feedback resulting from the SGID are compelling arguments in support of the SGID as the best method of gathering midsemester feedback.

Drawing on the categories of student comments appearing in past studies (Blue et al., 2014; Coffman, 1998; Newby et al., 1991; Sozer et al., 2019; Watson et al., 2018) and our own survey and interview research and from SGIDs that we each have conducted, Table 5.1 provides a snapshot of the major categories and types of feedback provided by students. Note that examples have been deliberately chosen to represent both affirming comments as well as suggestions for improvement. Although the examples

TABLE 5.1
Representative SGID Student Feedback

Category	Elements	Sample Student Comments—Helping or Hindering Learning
Instructor characteristics and behaviors	• availability • helpfulness and caring • enthusiasm for subject • subject knowledge • rapport with students • clarity of explanations	• authenticity • honesty • fun, cool-headed prof who treats us like adults • listens to all questions from students (students feel comfortable asking "stupid" questions) • encourages independence and autonomy • faster email replies • no digressions—stay on track • enjoy when you interact casually, less from notes • talk slower, particularly with technical terms
Instructional methods and assignments	• lectures • use of class time • expectations for in- and out-of-class work • course policies • group work • experiential opportunities • writing assignments	• open-ended discussion questions • good job splitting up the reading assignments so the reading load isn't too heavy • role-playing scenarios • uses multiple learning methods (group work, field work, lecture) • organize lectures better • spending more time explaining important concepts and not rushing through slides • better announcing upcoming assignments that are due • difficult to see when you write on the side of the whiteboard • we need more time to talk about work with peers

(Continued)

TABLE 5.1 (*Continued*)

Category	Elements	Sample Student Comments—Helping or Hindering Learning
Course content and materials	• textbook, readings • videos, digital learning objects • relevance, applicability • level of difficulty • pace • level of interest	• real-world stories • content builds and is thus easy to follow the progression • experiences/explanations of classmates • connecting final throughout the course (relevance) • videos are sometimes long and outdated • two textbooks conflict
Feedback and evaluation	• types of quizzes and exams • formative and summative feedback • grading practices • grading schema • help sessions and support available	• nongraded online quizzes • practice problems • lots of time for papers and the revision help • project rubric needed • exam review guide would be helpful • excel tutorial up front to help students less familiar with it • more opportunity for graded work
Student contributions to their own learning	• enthusiasm for subject • attendance and participation • completion of assignments • engagement with peers • engagement with instructor • engagement with support services	• stay on top of reading and homework (don't wait) • watch videos online • participate in class • weekly review of material learned • going to tutoring and instructor office hours

constitute the types of comments often provided, the ratio of affirming comments to suggestions for improvement is not necessarily representative of typical SGID feedback.

Studying the SGID

Since the early 1980s, evidence has been steadily accumulating in support of the SGID. The kinds of data typically gathered fall into several categories: (a) faculty satisfaction with the SGID, (b) instructor descriptions of course impact, (c) student satisfaction with the SGID, (d) student perceptions of the course, and (e) student learning. What we find somewhat curious, given the rather widespread nature of the method, is the paucity of SGID research. (In the course of working on this book, we have assembled many intriguing questions worthy of further investigation and will come back to this topic in chapter 8.) Generalizability of past published work is often confounded by the fact that studies are limited in scope (number of courses, instructors, and students) and the disciplines represented. Furthermore, the particular format of the SGID and the nature of who serves as consultant (colleague, educational developer, student) often vary. Nevertheless, we have observed the growth over the past few years in studies that utilize the SGID as a research tool, deploying the SGID to interrogate a curriculum reform project or adoption of a new teaching technique. We have included such studies here to illustrate the breadth of impact of the SGID.

As this chapter focuses primarily on what takes place over a limited time period—between midsemester and the end of the semester—and on the instructor and students in a particular course, the evidence of impact is similarly limited in scope. We fully recognize the burden of follow-up that is required to document longer term impacts of the SGID as well as the complexity in establishing a direct relationship between past SGIDs and future teaching improvements. We thus invite the reader, in reviewing what we know about the SGID from the perspective of the instructor and the students, to reflect upon the common themes that emerge and the rich portrait of productive learning environments that has been created through the study of the SGID.

From the Perspective of the Instructor

A substantial part of teaching is learning. And learning inherently involves change. An instructor curious about how a course is going opens themselves to the possibility of change. As educational developers, we have found the SGID to affect swift and meaningful change in ways that no other learning opportunity affords. There is no substitute for experience, and the real-time nature of the SGID means that it more closely can be described as on-the-job training for instructors as opposed to the learning that takes place by reading articles or books or attending a workshop (Katz & Henry, 1988). In fact, instructors surveyed about their SGID experience report that the experience was valuable and that the method of gathering feedback revealed aspects of the course that would have been missed in a simple survey or class observation (Craig, 2007; Diamond, 2004). In our own research, we heard time and again a similar message: The SGID provides instructors with timely, formative feedback from a highly credible source. Beyond instructor satisfaction with the SGID, what we have learned from instructors about the changes influenced by the SGID fall into three broad categories: an improved environment for learning, changes to teaching practices, and deepened critically reflective practices.

Improved Learning Environment

By having an SGID conducted in their course, an instructor is likely to notice a change in the classroom. The process has a natural tendency to break down barriers, resulting in better communication and enhanced rapport among all involved in the class (Clark & Redmond, 1982). An instructor may notice more hands going up during class discussion, a greater willingness of students to provide feedback about the course in other ways, and even more chatter among students before class starts. Rather than wondering what students are thinking, the SGID provides the instructor with new insights into the student perspective on the course (Diamond, 2004; Finelli et al., 2011). These benefits, of course, are predicated on the instructor closing the loop with students in a meaningful way, both affirming and acting upon their feedback (Abbott et al., 1990; Lewis, 2001; McDonnell & Dodd, 2017).

Changed Teaching Practices

Instructors overwhelmingly report that the SGID gave them new insights into their teaching, such that they planned to make changes based on the feedback. For example, Finelli et al. (2011) reported that 90% of instructors surveyed in their study indicated that they had made changes to their course as a result of the SGID. Revisions to teaching practices often include changed assignments, greater adoption of active learning strategies, clearer integration of homework and in-class activities, and presentation of more examples and practical applications of material (Diamond, 2004). Another common area of change involves clarification of expectations related to readings, assignments, and assessments. Even if an instructor explains the purpose of a group project on the 1st day of class or provides writing assignment rubrics as part of the course syllabus, is it possible that not every student is on the same page. The SGID feedback allows instructors to uncover disconnects between their intentions and students' understanding. We are certain that going into the

SGID, instructors do not necessarily appreciate the ways in which they will alter their teaching. Evidence suggests that in both small and large ways, an SGID results in changes to the course; in turn, instructors report an increase in student motivation and demonstrably improved attitude about the course and instructor (Mauger, 2010).

The SGID has also been used to inform teaching practices in a more directed way, providing instructors with valuable feedback about new curricula and new pedagogies. Several thorough studies have combined the SGID with other feedback mechanisms, helping instructors make informed decisions during a semester and over the course of several years. Watson et al. (2018) interrogated a new community-based microbiology capstone course with four SGIDs during a single semester. They used the feedback, alongside instructor reflections, assessment of student work, and SET data, to track the success of new pedagogies. Thematic analysis of the SGID results led to important course adjustments and also revealed student growth in confidence, self-direction, and self-reliance as the course progressed. For the instructors, awareness of these themes allowed them to be more effective coaches to students in subsequent capstone course offerings. In a related study, Sit and Brudzinski (2017) studied the impact of assignments incorporated in transitioning a course from face-to-face to online over the course of several years. Based on SGID feedback, instructors added software tutorials, revised discussion board prompts, and were also affirmed in utilizing the learning management systems to permit reattempts on online assignments and incorporation of video tutorials.

Deepened Critically Reflective Practice
An SGID can be considered a midsemester metacognitive pause for both the students and the instructor, providing a structured opportunity to reflect on what has transpired and what comes next. Our survey and interviews with educational developers cite faculty growth through critical reflection as a significant benefit of the SGID. For one, the SGID provides input from multiple sources beyond the instructor's own perception—from students and the consultant. Integrating these multiple perspectives and then responding to the feedback in a direct (and rather public) way with students reinforces the reflective learning cycle (Kolb, 2015). It is worth mentioning here a principle supported by the instructional consultation literature: The most impactful SGID experiences allow ample time for the post-SGID instructor–consultant conversation (Penny & Coe, 2004).

The SGID also affords an opportunity for building professional confidence. Instructors new to SGIDs are often surprised by the quantity and quality of students' comments. The balance of "helps learning" versus "hinders learning" feedback can catch them off guard. A preconceived image of a whiteboard filled with only things that the students don't like can be rather intimidating, we have been told. It can be a real morale boost when the SGID turns out to not be as bad as feared. One can imagine that this confidence propels the instructor toward a productive rest of the semester and a deeper respect and understanding for the students with whom they share the classroom. This confidence contributes to a sense of belonging to a community of educators and success in future semesters (Craig, 2007).

It is our sincere hope that the reflective practices fostered by the SGID come to bear as instructors review their end-of-semester SETs and also as they teach their future courses. Although others have reported that instructors find the SGID to be more helpful than SETs (Heppner & Johnston, 1994), SETs are a reality at most institutions. The approach to interpreting and responding to student feedback we have described for the SGID applies beautifully to making productive use of SET information. We would be remiss if we didn't mention the potential connection between SGIDs and SETs. Several studies have shown an improvement in student ratings for courses in which an SGID took place (Finelli et al., 2008; Wickramasinghe & Timpson, 2006). Gains also occur in indicators such as perception of the learning environment and instructor enthusiasm that are parallel to the improvements associated with other methods of soliciting midsemester feedback (McDonnell & Dodd, 2017; Piccinin, 1999). Recognizing that student feedback can come in a variety of forms, we conclude this section with an affirmation that, from the very instructors who've had them, the SGID is worth the time invested and deserves its frequent recommendation to colleagues (Finelli et al., 2008, 2011).

From the Perspective of the Students

Analyses of student feedback provided in SGID reports reveal common themes of strengths and areas for improvement for courses; the themes appear across disciplines and levels of courses. We are thrilled to be able to report that the course aspects that students identify as helping them learn align well with known elements of effective teaching and learning, including personal characteristics of the instructors such as perceived helpfulness, caring, and communication (Blue et al., 2014; Newby et al., 1991; Sozer et al., 2019). As further evidence that students engage authentically in the process, others have shown that students provide balanced feedback in terms of the number of comments that identify strengths versus areas for improvement (Coffman, 1998; Sozer et al., 2019). In addition to analyzing student feedback detailed in SGID reports, what we have learned from students about the impact of the SGID falls into three broad categories: an improved learning environment, engagement in the SGID process itself, and outcomes such as learning and motivation.

Improved Learning Environment

The positive contributions of the SGID to the learning environment we mentioned in the "From the Perspective of the Instructor" section are echoed by students. Students *really* appreciate the opportunity to provide feedback in this manner. Rapport with the instructor is improved in response to SGID participation because, not surprisingly, it is not lost on students that by engaging in the process, an instructor shows that they care about what students think and about their learning (Cook-Sather, 2009; Hurney et al., 2014; Wickramasinghe & Timpson, 2006). What students also notice, though, is the potential for an SGID to result in changes made during that semester. The instructor's receptivity and responsiveness to the feedback as well as the extent to which the instructor acts upon the feedback is important (Mauger, 2010; Redmond, 1982). The other aspect to an improved learning environment is stronger collegiality among the students following an SGID. Our favorite way we have heard this described is "I definitely feel like there [was] more of a sense that we all own the class a little more" (Cook-Sather, 2009, p. 237).

Engagement in the SGID

Both undergraduate and graduate students respond overwhelmingly positively when asked about the experience of having participated in an SGID and also nearly universally consider the SGID more helpful than SETs (Abbott et al., 1990; Heppner & Johnston, 1994; Mauger, 2010). When asked to provide specific benefits of the SGID, students comment on the opportunity to provide feedback and hear the perspectives of their peers (Redmond, 1982; Sherry et al., 1998; Wulff et al., 1985). Similar to what instructors describe as the benefits of an SGID, students also note the improved learning environment as well as better attitudes toward the course and the instructor (Mauger, 2010). We have witnessed the positive response of students to being asked to engage in an SGID and can attest to the fact that students recommend that other instructors use the process to gather feedback (Mauger, 2010; Redmond, 1982; Wulff et al., 1985). Others have reported positive outcomes based on the inherently collaborative, public, interactive, and still anonymous nature of the SGID, including higher quality feedback and enhanced engagement with the process (Sherry et al., 1998; Veeck et al., 2016).

Sidebar: Not a semester goes by where a student doesn't come up to me after I conduct an SGID and ask me how they can request an SGID be carried out in another instructor's class. I go to great lengths as part of my introductory remarks to let the students know that the SGID was requested voluntarily by their instructor, hoping that my statements situate the SGID in the context of an instructor's own quest to ensure a quality learning experience. Nevertheless, student interest in our SGID program has led to some awkward moments. When I am approached by a student (or a group of students) at the whiteboard as I am erasing their comments, I remind them that the instructor needs to request the SGID from our center during a certain window of the semester. I do encourage the students to share information about the SGID with their instructors, but the eyerolls tell me that they are unlikely to do something that might appear to challenge the instructor. I don't blame them. We have also had student interest in the SGID surface during faculty workshops about midsemester feedback. These particular workshops are the only ones for which we generate student interest in attendance. Although not advertised to students, over the years, students have come, wanting to contribute to the conversation. The students have always been welcomed and have added their voice to the importance of asking students for midsemester feedback, particularly via an SGID. But I have to say that on our campus, we have not yet arrived at a way for students to request or nominate an instructor for an SGID.—Christine M. Rener

Learning and Learning-Oriented Behaviors

Through participation in an SGID, a student engages in a process that can benefit themselves as learners and as members of a class. First and foremost, the metacognitive pause provides an opportunity to reflect on the course goals, their own contributions to their own learning as well as that of their peers, and the intentions of the instruction as well as the perceptions of their peers. Some of the most gratifying aspects of the SGID in the authors' experience have been the instances wherein students, upon hearing the comments of other students in the class, have resolved their own misconceptions about the course (*The readings are listed in the syllabus? A study guide is posted online?*).

In terms of other learning-associated impacts of the SGID, Redmond (1982) reported an increase in motivation for students who participated in an SGID. A self-report questionnaire asked students to rate their participation and engagement with the course materials, among other items. At the end of the semester, relative to students who had not experienced an SGID, study participants in the SGID had significantly improved in many motivation-related behaviors. Imagine the sense of satisfaction and validation for a student who, in providing a specific piece of feedback about course structure, sees that very change in place for the remainder of the semester. In a more recent study looking at the impact of the SGID on students, Hurney et al. (2014) found an increase in student motivation, enthusiasm, and behaviors indicative of taking more responsibility for their own learning (e.g., studying, participating, managing time). More importantly, this impact was significantly higher when the following learner-centered questions were incorporated into the SGID:

1. What are *you* doing to help your learning in this course?
2. What are *you* doing to hinder your learning in this course?
3. What could *you* do to improve your learning in this course?

These questions have now become routinely incorporated into our own SGID programs, as in many others. We firmly believe in the importance of reflective practices for instructors and certainly for students; the SGID provides an ideal venue for activating metacognition for all involved.

Although it is implied that learning will be altered as a result of having an SGID in a course, the direct evidence for this is, so far, sparse. This might seem like a strange state of affairs, given that Redmond's (1982) work—among the first empirical examinations of SGIDs—examined self-reported motivation for learning. But psychologists have long been aware of the disconnect that can exist between student motivation and behavioral performance, and are wary of assuming that motivation necessarily begets learning. Perhaps this relative dearth of evidence for the impact of SGIDs on learning exists because research in educational development typically examines instructors rather than students. Or perhaps it exists because measuring learning is both a difficult and laborious process, and one that often requires elaborate methodological approaches. Nevertheless, we hope that future work in SGID will take up the mantle to provide more compelling and direct evidence of SGIDs on student learning. Such studies might involve comparing learning artifacts before and after an SGID, or comparisons across similar courses (such as introductory-level courses) with and without SGIDs.

Making the Case for SGIDs to Instructors and Other Interested Parties

The chapter has detailed the evidence that supports the overwhelmingly compelling nature of what students have to say and what can be learned by providing students with an opportunity for open-ended feedback. If someone asked me to share convincing evidence—whether an individual instructor considering an SGID for the first time or an administrator looking to jump-start an evidence-based teaching-focused initiative—what would be the short list of supporting literature I might provide? In the citations to the following, we have outlined more of a snapshot rather than a comprehensive list, but it might prove useful to have these papers handy to share. Speaking from experience, the ability to draw upon these papers has helped us on our own campuses. From our survey data and our own experiences, faculty resistance has been a barrier to wider implementation of SGIDs. Particular concerns include a lack of perceived value, an unwillingness to devote class time, and a general unfamiliarity with the practice. To help you respond to similar concerns and make the case, consider the following.

Do Instructors Report the SGID to Be a Valuable Experience?

- Instructors report gaining insights into student perspectives about the course, making substantive adjustments to their teaching, and carrying over those changes to subsequent course offerings (Diamond, 2004).
- Instructors report that the SGID encourages reflection, helps identify specific areas of teaching improvement, results in course changes, is worth the time invested, and is worthy of recommendation to colleagues, with an added bonus—gains in end-of-semester ratings (Finelli et al., 2008).

What Kinds of Feedback Do Students Provide During an SGID?

- Coding analyses of SGID reports reveal common themes of strengths and areas for improvement in the student feedback; the aspects of a course that students identify as helping them learn align well with known elements of effective teaching and learning (Blue et al., 2014; Sozer et al., 2019).
- Common themes in student comments are seen across disciplines and levels of courses; students provide balanced feedback in terms of the number of comments that identify strengths versus areas for improvement (Coffman, 1998; Sozer et al., 2019).

Do Students Find the SGID to Be a Valuable Way to Provide Feedback?

- Both undergraduate and graduate students respond overwhelmingly positively when asked about participating in an SGID and also nearly universally consider the SGID more helpful than SETs (Abbott et al., 1990; Heppner & Johnston, 1994; Mauger, 2010).
- End-of-semester ratings reflect improvements in the perceptions of the instructor, course, and their own learning, suggesting that the SGID positively impacted the student experience (Finelli et al., 2008).

Although captured to some extent by student surveys and interviews, the most striking benefit of the SGID to us is the way in which students have an impactful avenue for providing feedback about a course. As consultants, we have been in the same room with students who express gratitude to us for our efforts and also express profound appreciation that their instructor cared enough to ask for their feedback in this way. These experiences buoy our resolve as to the powerful impact of the SGID on everyone involved in a course. In chapter 6, we turn our attention to the impact of the SGID beyond the instructor and student. We widen the sphere of influence to consider the SGID consultant, the academic department or program, the CTL, and finally, the institution itself. Relying less on prior research, we will take a narrative, case-based approach to rounding out the picture of the current and potential significance of the SGID.

6

THE IMPACT OF THE SGID
BEYOND THE COURSE

One of the signature programs offered by our CTL is a faculty mentoring program, providing, in part, small group mentoring opportunities for new faculty. Groups of 5–10 new faculty from varying disciplines meet with an experienced faculty mentor on a biweekly basis over either the 1st semester or 1st year (depending on schedules and interest). The curriculum for this program—what we call First Year Faculty Mentoring Communities—provides an introduction to faculty and student support services available at the university and addresses teaching topics timed to the rhythm of the semester. New faculty are strongly encouraged by their mentors to seek midsemester feedback from their students and the SGID is promoted as a voluntary opportunity to consider. A good number of new faculty do request an SGID, if not during their 1st semester, then certainly in advance of their first pretenure or contract renewal review. We particularly appreciate hearing from new faculty who report that several of the members of their First Year Faculty Mentoring Community decided to have an SGID and then came back to the group to compare notes. Although I haven't been in the room during those discussions, I am confident that everyone was in some way affirmed in what they were doing and also that they reported learning from the students and the consultant during the process.

One way that I know that these SGID experiences are having an impact is when we receive an SGID request from an instructor who indicates on the request form that they were motivated to request the SGID based on a recommendation from a newer faculty member in their department. In some cases, I have come to learn that the recommendation came through a casual conversation among colleagues or through a formal departmental mentoring relationship. In some instances, the SGID came to the attention of a more senior colleague through the personnel review process and seeing the ways in which the junior faculty member reflected on learning from the SGID. Over the years, our center has refined our data management practices and can more easily track participation of instructors in our programs. We find the SGID to be serving an interesting role—not only do the highly engaged instructors whom I would call our "usual suspects" request SGIDs, but those who engage in SGIDs often go on to participate in other center programs, such as non-SGID consultations and faculty learning communities.

For the SGIDs for which I have served as consultant, I can attest to the inter-est that instructors express in having continued conversations about teaching. Particularly in community with other instructors, these explorations are some-times the first time an instructor has dug into their teaching in a way sometimes only seen for scholarly pursuits. So although I am thrilled that the SGID has served in some cases as an entrée into further engagement in our center, I am even more gratified to have evidence of the power of the student voice to deepen an instructor's commitment to working on their teaching.

—Christine M. Rener

The previous chapter focused primarily on the impact of the SGID on individual courses, from the perspectives of the instructor and the students. In this chapter, we will examine a wide range of promising outcomes drawn from our own experience and those found in the literature, looking beyond the classroom and considering the SGID consultants, CTLs, academic departments, and institutions (Figure 6.1). What we will explore here is the ways in which even those not directly involved in the SGID can be positively impacted by simply having SGIDs carried out on campus. Even for an institution without a large SGID program, simply having more conversations about teaching and learning on a campus—among instructors and students—holds promise for positively influencing campus culture.

Another way to consider the multilevel impacts of the SGID is the evidence of impact model developed by Harper et al. (2020). Although the initial context of this framework (Figure 6.2) is the health and social

Figure 6.1. The six levels of impact of the SGID.

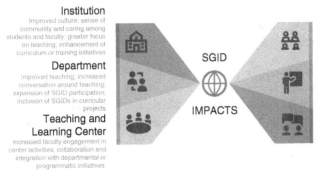

Institution
Improved culture; sense of community and caring among students and faculty; greater focus on teaching; enhancement of curriculum or training initiatives

Department
Improved teaching; increased conversation around teaching; expansion of SGID participation; inclusion of SGIDs in curricular projects

Teaching and Learning Center
Increased faculty engagement in center activities; collaboration and integration with departmental or programmatic initiatives

SGID

IMPACTS

Students
Reflection on their learning; enhanced communication with instructor and peers; ability to provide timely feedback and influence change; increased motivation; sense of caring and community

Instructor
Rich, detailed, and timely feedback; new insights into teaching practices as well as students; enhanced communication with students

Consultant
Perspective on one's own teaching; exposure to new teaching practices; increased empathy for students and faculty

Note. © Copyright PresentationGO.com. Graphic adapted with permission.

Figure 6.2. The evidence of impact model.

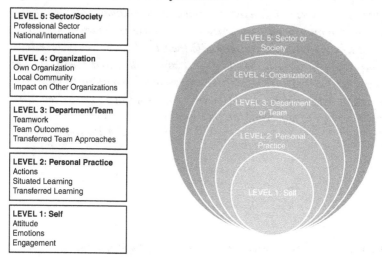

LEVEL 5: Sector/Society
Professional Sector
National/International

LEVEL 4: Organization
Own Organization
Local Community
Impact on Other Organizations

LEVEL 3: Department/Team
Teamwork
Team Outcomes
Transferred Team Approaches

LEVEL 2: Personal Practice
Actions
Situated Learning
Transferred Learning

LEVEL 1: Self
Attitude
Emotions
Engagement

Note. Adapted from Harper et al. (2020). Licensed under CC BY 4.0.

care sector, the applications to a higher education (and educational development) context appear helpful to us. The "self" in our case is the instructor. The particular attributes shown in Figure 6.2 of "attitude, emotions, and engagement" very much resonate with our aspirations for instructors involved in an SGID. We have witnessed a shift in attitudes toward students but also to the instructor's role in the learning process. The act of participating in all conversations of the SGID is an emotional process, at the very least eliciting a vulnerability that is not an easy space for everyone. Harper et al. further described this level of impact as involving not only personal satisfaction but also an individual feeling supported, seeing new perspectives, and gaining enhanced understanding. These very same ideas are used by instructors in describing the impact of the SGID on their teaching (see chapter 5). What is learned in an SGID is not meaningful unless put into practice (Level 2: Personal Practice in Figure 6.2) in the current course but also in future courses. This chapter will build on these levels of impact to explore an ever-widening circle of impact.

Impact of the SGID on the Consultant

Individuals serving as SGID consultants can hold a variety of other roles: educational developer, departmental colleague, nondepartmental peer, graduate student, or undergraduate student (Cook-Sather, 2009; Snooks et al., 2004). For any consultant, it is a privilege to be invited into a rather private space—normally reserved for the instructor and the students—and hear what really matters to everyone involved. In considering the impact of the experience on the consultant, it is worth taking time to consider the ways in which the SGID blurs individual roles during the four SGID conversations and necessitates a degree of vulnerability for all involved. At various stages, who serves primarily as learner, instructor, and consultant can vary. For example, the instructor occupies the role of learner as they consider their students' feedback and talk with the consultant. The students themselves serve as consultants to their instructors in providing their perspectives via the SGID. The consultant balances multiple roles over the course of the SGID and can thus be impacted in significant, layered ways. Interestingly, in our SGID survey, when we asked educational developers about methods of evaluation for SGID programs, one of the least often selected options was "impact on SGID consultants"; clearly, there is potential to explore this idea further.

Through the process of conducting an SGID, the consultant is afforded the opportunity to experience how others teach, gaining a unique new perspective on their own teaching and in the process learning more deeply about how students view various aspects of a class structure (Snooks et al., 2004). For both instructors and educational developers, the SGID provides an opportunity to learn about teaching, whether it be to hear about new or different teaching strategies, or to hear what students think about certain kinds of learning experiences. For example, what I learned through SGID consultations within the past year has inspired me to incorporate mastery grading, public poster sessions, and several new educational technologies into my own courses.

> **Sidebar:** I have learned so much through my experiences as an SGID consultant and I am certainly a better teacher because of every student and instructor who opened up their views of teaching and learning to me during the SGID conversations. But I am also a *much* better educational developer because of the SGID. The SGID is one of the only programs offered by the centers I have worked for that allows me to have direct contact with the students. Through the SGID I gained valuable perspectives about the academic cultures at the University of Virginia, James Madison University, and Colby College. Interacting with students within the context of the SGID helped me understand how students perceived the learning endeavor and how that impacted their perceptions of their instructors and courses. Talking with students about teaching and learning also helped me contextualize the work of the center and helped me develop better programs that included insights on how students viewed courses in various disciplines and how, at the end of the day, the kind of course didn't matter as much as the ways the instructors designed the courses, communicated expectations to the students, and created a welcoming environment for learning.—Carol A. Hurney

Two points in time during the SGID hold the potential to impact the consultant in particular and distinct ways: during the classroom conversation with students (Conversation 2; see especially the italicized quotes in the introduction) and also the debrief with the instructor (Conversation 3). Let's begin with the consultant interaction with the students. Simply witnessing positive student feedback about the course and enthusiastic engagement in the process can be uplifting and humbling (including the occasional eruption of applause at the conclusion of the session in celebration of the SGID experience and gratitude toward the consultant). Walking into a course that isn't going particularly well can be stressful and challenging to navigate smoothly. (In our experiences, this latter situation is rare; we have found that students overwhelmingly take the process seriously and provide constructive input.) Serving as an SGID consultant can be an exercise in empathy building and wrestling with the temptation to sometimes jump in and defend the instructor's approach or school the students on their reactions (see chapter 3 for guiding principles for SGID conversations and chapters 4 and 7 for discussion of consultant training). During discussion of the students' comments, the consultant must also balance gathering consensus perspectives with identifying and capturing minority viewpoints. In our SGID programs, we have found that the experience of managing these situations has helped instructors and educational developers serving as SGID consultants to hone their listening abilities, their openness to divergent perspectives, and their skillfulness in discussion facilitation. We would be hard pressed to cite an example where a consultant did not come away from an SGID with renewed respect for the ability of students to provide substantive, authentic feedback. Although we do not have students serving as consultants on our campuses, similar outcomes have been noted for student-led SGIDs (Cox & Sorenson, 2000).

Turning next to Conversation 3—the debrief between the consultant and instructor wherein the consultant reports on the student feedback and provides suggestions for moving forward—we find the consultant flexing slightly different skills. Clark and Redmond (1982) have described a taxonomy of consultant roles important in this moment: communication channel (from students to instructor), information source (sharing additional resources), and interpreter (providing potential explanations for students' comments). In serving as a communication channel, a consultant is tasked with elevating students' voices with impartiality, potentially in the face of some instructor resistance. Managing this part of the conversation has been noted as a particular challenge for students serving as consultants (Cook-Sather, 2009; see also "The Student-Led SGID" section in chapter 2). As the conversation turns to responding to student feedback and approaching the remainder of the semester, the consultant has a responsibility to represent

---

Sidebar: One of the things that I've found really compelling about SGIDs is the way that the consultant can help guide students toward providing better, more actionable feedback. Perhaps because they are often on the receiving end of feedback, students often do not have a lot of experience at giving effective feedback. But SGIDs allow students to practice this. With the guidance of a consultant, students learn how to provide action-able feedback (*The readings are really complex in this course; I wish there was some way the instructor could provide some pointers about what information we should take away from them*) instead of nonactionable feedback (*This course is hard*). In fact, often the conversations early in SGID sessions start with students providing this kind of nonactionable feedback, but with finesse, the consultant can help draw out the perspectives that students have that are actionable and will improve their course. Students then come to realize that certain feedback just isn't helpful for making changes to a course; it can describe how they feel, but not how to correct a ship that's heading off course. With enough practice, students can develop an understanding of how to provide this helpful feedback, which will benefit them in all kinds of ways (e.g., when working with teams, when working with supervisors or subordinates).—Jordan D. Troisi

---

teaching and learning best practices and offer suggestions from a position of some knowledge. Granted, this last point might apply most to educational developers serving as consultants with the backdrop of representing their CTL. Another aspect of this conversation dynamic, noted by one of our interviewees, is the need to meet the instructor where they are and attend to their needs. Suffice it to say, an awareness of the various levels of meaning during this conversation helps individuals develop their interpersonal and consultation abilities.

From the perspective of all three authors of this book, serving as an SGID consultant is one of the most rewarding roles that we have engaged in our educational development roles. When asked about the impact of the SGID on consultants, our survey and interviews surfaced words such as *enriching, rewarding, connecting, enjoyable, powerful, satisfying*. We couldn't agree more.

Impact of the SGID on CTLs

The SGID provides a valuable service in itself in addition to serving as a most benevolent gateway to further engagement with the expertise of our centers. For those coordinating educational development efforts, under the aegis of a CTL or not, an SGID program can result in greater instructor participation in education development programs of all types. We have experienced increased instructor engagement with our centers in the semester following an SGID, repeated requests for SGIDs (particularly from those instructors experimenting with a new pedagogy or teaching strategy), as well as word-of-mouth referrals from colleagues within a department.

Of the 229 respondents to our SGID survey of educational developers, 63% (n = 145) conduct SGIDs on their campuses. In narrative comments as well as during our set of follow-up interviews, participants often cited strengthened center engagement as a benefit of having an SGID program. Whether the SGID serves as either an easy first point of contact with the center or entrée to a deeper collaboration, the theme of relationships should not be overlooked. Building upon a trusting, reciprocal relationship between instructor and educational developer (Taylor et al., 2020), a positive experience with an SGID consultation can open the doors for instructors to not only feel comfortable working with a center in another capacity but to recommend that peers do the same.

In addition to stand-alone SGID programs, CTLs have seen value in incorporating the SGID into other educational development activities. For example, new instructors or teaching assistants can experience the SGID as part of an orientation or training program (Black, 1998). At Grand Valley State University, the SGID has been offered as a component of new faculty mentoring groups and an Inclusive Excellence Teaching Institute. We have also experienced clusters of SGID requests from groups of faculty involved in projects such as departmental curricular revisions or senior faculty mentoring groups. It speaks to the reputation of the center and the perceived value of the SGID that instructors engage as part of collaborative projects such as these.

The SGID also holds the potential to impact center programming in either direct or indirect ways. Analysis of themes revealed in SGID reports—identifying common student frustrations, for example—could help direct center efforts. As Sozer et al. (2019) described, in response to teaching challenges identified through a qualitative analysis of SGID reports, their CTL increased programming around topics such as learning management system use and use of student response systems. At Grand Valley State University, during our SGID program pilot year, we learned that not as many instructors as we had thought were making a regular practice of gathering midsemester feedback in their courses. This observation, in concert with the strong favorable student response to participating in SGIDs, compelled us to offer workshops promoting wider midsemester feedback practices. We presented evidence supporting collecting student feedback, detailed a range of methods, and, of course, promoted our new SGID opportunity.

For centers looking for clever ways to engage more instructors in SGIDs—or for those considering launching an SGID program—we have drawn inspiration from two studies describing a center's deployment of the SGID in an unusual way. In the first, the SGID format was used with instructors participating in a student feedback best practices workshop, wherein the instructors themselves engaged in an SGID, addressing prompts related to instructor perceptions of SETs (Blash et al., 2018). The workshop facilitators gained valuable information and the instructors were introduced to the SGID. Another project that engaged instructors themselves in an SGID involved a project related to the program-wide adoption of team-based learning. The SGID was pressed into service in probing instructor perception of their own implementation of the pedagogy (Remington et al., 2015). Suffice it to say, although the SGID is great for midsemester feedback, it's also great for many more purposes as well.

Impact of the SGID on the Department or Program

The next institutional context for which an SGID can have an impact is an academic department or program. The SGID can contribute to a thriving departmental culture—one that explicitly values teaching. Coming back again to the evidence of impact model (Figure 6.2), Level 3 describes the impact of a program at the departmental or team level; descriptors of Level 3 include greater teamwork practices and transfer of collaborative approaches to other settings (Harper et al., 2020). I don't know of a higher education institution that couldn't benefit from academic departments or programs working more closely together as teams of equal peers or for instructors to carry out shared work (e.g., as part of faculty governance committees) with greater collaborative adeptness. Having the SGID serve in some respects as a catalyst for increased departmental cohesiveness and functioning is an exciting prospect to us and one that is borne out in the literature, in our own study, as well as in our experiences on multiple campuses. In addition to functioning well as a unit, most, if not all, departments want to ensure high-quality teaching and student learning throughout their programs. Importantly, an SGID does not only impact a single course but instructors who have participated in SGIDs report that they anticipate carrying changes over to subsequent offerings of the class (Diamond, 2004; Finelli et al., 2011; Heppner & Johnston, 1994).

One way to explicitly demonstrate that a department or program values teaching is to "simply" talk more about teaching. The SGID can be part of this conversation, whether among instructors or graduate student teaching assistants. Craig (2007) noted how instructors reported sharing their SGID reports with others and included SGID reports in annual activity reports and personnel portfolios. We have seen similar practices on our own campuses, wherein faculty are comfortable talking about the fact that they had SGIDs with their peers or department chair. We are also hopeful that some of the challenges identified in our survey data around awareness of SGID programs and instructor resistance related to lack of perceived value and time commitment can be overcome at the department level as instructors share more widely. On a cautionary note, we would not want to see departments move toward expectations for instructor engagement in SGIDs or overreliance on SGID information in personnel decisions. Maintaining the formative nature of the SGID is of the utmost importance and we would encourage all engaged in SGIDs—either at the level of the individual instructor to those in administrative positions—to moderate expectations for instructional improvement and direct impact on SET results.

Within a department, we might reasonably imagine the practice spreading as instructors share favorable SGID experiences and recommend them to other colleagues. Although word of mouth is wonderful, integrating the SGID into a departmental or programmatic initiative can yield even greater benefit. The SGID can provide important formative feedback within departmental curricular projects such as introductory course revisions or a general education refresh. Deployment of the SGID across multiple classes such that the collective feedback is shared with instructors for discussion is an opportunity for even greater impact. As mentioned in chapters 3 and 4, the success of such approaches hinges on a shared understanding of issues of confidentiality, the exclusively formative nature of the SGID, and inherent power dynamics among faculty (and students).

We have seen several compelling ways in which the SGID has been used to inform collaborative curriculum projects. For example, Watson et al. (2018) described a capstone redesign initiative for which the SGID was used to collect student impressions four times over the course of the semester. The instructors were able to affirm their design—incorporating problem-based and service-learning components—but also make adjustments along the way. Longer lasting impacts of the investigation included increasing the credit hours of the course, outfitting a support laboratory, and instructors reporting being able to better serve as learning coaches for future students. Interestingly, the SGID student feedback served to help legitimize the course in the face of department and university skepticism. In another curriculum reform project, this time related to incorporation of team-based learning across a set of courses within a program, Remington et al. (2015) described the benefits of SGIDs on the instructors involved. As instructors brought SGID feedback into the planning committee discussions, instructors who had not yet taught their team-based learning courses were able to adjust their plans in response to the students' comments.

Impact of the SGID on the Institution

The final aspect of SGID impact that we would like the reader to consider is the institution itself, represented in the evidence of impact model as Level 4 (Figure 6.2). The kinds of institution-level impacts that we can imagine the SGID having range from the less tangible to the perhaps more tangible. In our survey of educational developers, "campus academic culture" was rarely a measure of SGID outcomes. Nonetheless, there are three distinct ways that we can envision the SGID having an impact beyond the individuals involved and even a particular academic department program or department. Despite the limited evidence collected to date, we are firm in our conviction of the potential of the SGID to improve the overall culture of an institution around teaching and learning: not only talking about teaching but committing to continued efforts to improve teaching. SGIDs can also serve as part of larger institutional initiatives—around inclusive teaching or general education reform, for example. Lastly, the ripple effect of a sense of belonging among instructors and students fostered by participation on SGIDs can only strengthen an institution's community.

Teaching and Learning Culture

Despite our shared commitment to our students and to the enterprise of learning, not all institutions have a culture that values public discourse about teaching. Often as a more private endeavor, instructors close their classroom doors (literally or figuratively) and toil in silence. Although that imagery might be an exaggeration, we have seen throughout our own academic careers that one's teaching successes and failures are not a typical topic of conversation around campus. As greater numbers of instructors participate in SGIDs, the normalization of a culture of inquiry around teaching could very well follow. So, not only discussing with others—peers, staff, students— what is happening in one's classes, but also what is working well and what is still a source of frustration would represent a culture shift. Greater openness to both giving and receiving good feedback would benefit instructors and students alike. Despite a great deal of time and effort spent around assessing student learning and engaging in quality assurance projects, we don't have a lot of evidence that our institutions exhibit the hallmarks of a culture of continuous improvement. Maybe rightly so, assessment efforts focus on *student* learning and not necessarily *faculty* learning. In our research, we were heartened to see mention of having an SGID program as instilling a culture of formative assessment at a large research university, in one case, and a culture of learning, in another. Even in the absence of a direct link, we do view the SGID as a potent promoter of a culture with greater emphasis on the act of teaching and learning about teaching.

Institutional Priorities

The SGID is ideally suited to furthering institutional priorities such as teaching improvement in university-wide programs such as general education, community-based learning programs, or inclusive teaching initiatives. Reaching beyond a single department or program, such projects could be informed by SGIDs used either by individual instructors for their own benefit or as part of group conversations about the progress of curricular changes. Having rich formative feedback while engaged in course improvement projects such as this makes the SGID an ideal activity to build into the initiative. An additional benefit, in our experience, has been that instructors bring the SGID back to their home department, requesting SGIDs in courses not part of the institutional initiative and encouraging their disciplinary colleagues to give it a try. To better capture this ripple effect, we recommend including a further question on SGID request forms: *How did you hear about the SGID?*

Another approach to making use of the SGID at the institutional level is to conduct a thematic analysis of SGID reports, as carried out by Sozer et al. in 2018. Analyzing themes that emerged from campus-wide SGIDs were used in this study to inform CTL programming. How else could such an analysis prove useful? Depending on the particular institutional priority or initiative, SGID information could prove diagnostic, supportive, or even inspirational. For example, we could envision SGIDs revealing the extent to which students report project-based learning experiences to help their learning, lending support for adoption of a consistent learning management system across campus or stimulating greater participation of instructors in inclusive teaching practices workshops. Any such projects would need to be carried out with utmost sensitivity to protecting instructor and student privacy, but this type of practice is frequently done in the realm of the scholarship of teaching and learning (SoTL) under the auspices of an institutional review board (IRB). As institutions with wider SGID adoption plan what happens next, such large-scale analyses could prove useful to consider.

Sense of Community

Earlier in this chapter, we mentioned the sense of community, both in classrooms and departments fostered by SGID participation. Going one step further, we can readily envision a profound impact of the SGID on a sense of community, belonging, and caring among students and instructors at the level of the institution. Even in cases where SGID engagement is not particularly systematic, the benefits to the institution can be similarly profound. Students, as well as instructors, report a greater sense of caring, belonging, and community as a result of participation in an SGID (e.g., Clark & Redmond, 1982; Hunt, 2003; Wulff et al., 1985). Students feel respected and valued for having been asked their perspectives, appreciating that their instructor cares and is committed to the students' learning enough to take class time to engage with the protocol. We think it is worth mentioning that *all* students should understand that their instructors care deeply about their learning. Unfortunately, without explicitly stating so, instructors sometimes miss the opportunity to connect with their students at a deeper level than over the course content. Over the series of post-SGID conversations, consultants often become aware of how deeply an instructor cares about their students and how hard they work to ensure their students are learning. The SGID itself becomes a manifestation of this caring, communicating to students that the instructor values their perspectives and is committed to incorporating their feedback into the course moving forward.

For instructors, the SGID has the potential to build community with colleagues and reduce the sense of isolation (Snooks et al., 2004). Whether facilitated by an educational developer or a peer, an SGID can be a rare opportunity for an instructor to engage in an authentic conversation about their teaching and their students' learning. These peer-to-peer conversations can be impactful, particularly when the SGID is fully realized as a trust-requiring and trust-building exercise—on the part of the instructor *and* the students. In an ideal world, our academic communities would be suffused with engaging conversations about teaching and learning—among instructors, students, early career faculty, graduate student instructors, and between instructors and students. The SGID is the ideal mechanism to stimulate and/or continue such conversations—taking place at the right time and engaging those who matter most—the instructor and the students.

Impact of the SGID Beyond the Institution

There certainly may be other ways that we have not yet considered for the intentional leveraging of SGIDs to support particular institutional priorities and to have impact at varying levels within our institutions. We hope that you have been inspired to think about the SGID in ways beyond a single classroom. The final level of the evidence of impact model—Level 5 in Figure 6.2—invites us to consider impact beyond our institutions, to our sectors and to wider society. Thinking about the local, national, and international potential for the impact of an SGID practice or program immediately calls SoTL to mind for us. Documenting and disseminating not only the impacts of the SGID itself but deploying the SGID as a research tool are the natural next steps to us. In chapter 8, about SGID research, the reader will find practical guidance for carrying out SGID-related SoTL and for applying the "gold standards for SoTL" to your own SGID project.

PART FOUR

MAXIMIZING THE POTENTIAL

7

ENHANCING THE SGID
AND SGID PROGRAMS

In the mid-2000s, my SGID team at James Madison University began to notice that students were only focused on the role of the instructor when providing their feedback during the SGID. We had been using a traditional three-question set that asked students to indicate what helped their learning, what hindered their learning, and what suggestions they had to improve learning. They would sometimes provide details about their role in the course, but often, even though we prompted them to think holistically about the course, their answers to what helped and hindered learning were all about what the instructor was doing to help and hinder learning. To remedy this, we added a set of questions that directly challenged the students to reflect on their role in the course—what were they doing to help learning, what were they doing to hinder learning, and what could they do to improve learning.

These questions changed everything. At first we didn't set up a study to examine the impact of the new questions; we simply decided to give these new questions a try. I knew in the middle of the first SGID I did with the new questions that something different was happening during both the conversations students were having with each other and then with me. I came rushing back to the center after doing my first SGID using the new questions, eager to tell my colleagues about the transformation. They were excited, but skeptical. But soon all of the consultants were expressing how the addition of these metacognitive questions contextualized the SGID feedback by providing insights into student behaviors—the good, the bad, and the ugly. Students told us that they were forming study groups and going to office hours. But they also told us that they didn't read the book or that they were just skimming the reading for answers to discussion questions or quizzes. And they also revealed that sometimes they were not paying attention in class or that they were texting or using social media. The raw honesty of their feedback about their own behaviors, though a little unsettling, was refreshing. We were impressed by how the additional feedback improved all of the SGID conversations by painting a clearer picture of both sides of the teaching and learning equation.

We went on to test the impact of these questions by designing a controlled study comparing the new learner-centered SGID with the traditional SGID

(Hurney et al., 2014). Our results demonstrated that a statistically significant number of students who experienced the learner-centered SGID reported making positive changes to their study behaviors as a result of the experience. Additionally, we found that students who experienced the learner-centered SGID reported a better understanding of course assignments, more interactions with classmates, increased motivation to excel, and more enthusiasm for the course.

From my perspective as a consultant, the real impact of the learner-centered SGID questions is how the feedback from the students about their own invest-ment in the course changes how the instructor views the feedback, giving them insights into the behaviors that their midcourse corrections can directly address. In the end, adding three questions to our SGID protocol enhanced all of the SGID conversations, resulting in midcourse corrections that impacted both instructor and student behaviors.

—Carol A. Hurney

E stablishing an effective SGID experience or program begins by follow-ing the guidelines we provide throughout this book. Getting the SGID experience to more instructors, to inform more midcourse correc-tion experiences, involves getting the SGID integrated into the institutional culture in ways that support the confidential, formative feedback instructors can use to inform midcourse corrections and course design. Enhancing the impact of the SGID experience requires intentional reflection about each element of the SGID, how these elements can support pedagogical change, and ways to integrate the SGID into broader strategic planning initiatives. In this chapter we focus on expanding the reach of the SGID across the institu-tion, enhancing consultant training to support better SGID conversations, improving the ways SGID results inform course corrections, and creating spaces for dialogue about the SGID and SGID results.

Expanding the Reach of the SGID

The reach of your SGID program reflects the number of SGIDs your group or program conducts each semester and the demographics of the instruc-tors who engage with this midcourse feedback experience (e.g., rank, depart-ment). Both aspects of program reach—number of SGIDs and participant demographics—relate directly to the capacity of your group or program to offer SGIDs and to the marketing strategies used to inform instructors of the value of the SGID.

Increasing SGID capacity involves growing your SGID consultant pool. The best pool of recruits are faculty who have experienced the SGID process in one of their courses, because they have firsthand knowledge of the kind of feedback students provide and the ways the SGID impacted the learning experience in their classes. However, although most faculty are equipped to facilitate the first two SGID conversations with the students, not all faculty have enough teaching or consulting experience to effectively debrief with the faculty member regarding the SGID results (SGID Conversation 3). There is some good news here, as we discussed in chapter 3, in that most faculty can be trained to provide an effective conversation with faculty, but it takes time for these faculty to fully realize their potential in the SGID consultant role. Another pool of recruits are faculty who have taken on administrative roles at your institutions, such as program directors or department chairs. These faculty have a bigger picture view of the teaching culture at your institution and often have some experience mentoring faculty in their areas. Finally, you can also engage faculty emeriti to join your SGID consultant pool, as these faculty have extensive teaching experience, flexible schedules, and are passionate about student learning.

Many centers have extended the reach of their SGID programs by welcoming graduate and undergraduate student consultants into the SGID program (Black, 1998). Graduate students are an excellent source of SGID consultants due to their role as instructors at many institutions. Graduate students bring new ideas about teaching to the SGID process. In addition, being an SGID consultant complements their training as future faculty, providing deeper insights into teaching and learning issues, while also giving them experience working with CTLs. Integrating undergraduate students as consultants embraces a growing trend to welcome undergraduates into educational development programs as pedagogical partners (Cook-Sather et al., 2014). Moreover, student consultants offer insights into the teaching and learning endeavor while also being more approachable for students during the classroom SGID conversations. Integrating students into the SGID makes transparent to the students how faculty engage in the course design process. Faculty also benefit by empowering the student voice—both of the student consultants and of the students in their courses. Introducing students as pedagogical partners in the midcourse feedback process fills a relationship gap, allowing faculty and students to engage as colleagues, working together to interpret and respond to SGID feedback. Engaging student consultants in the SGID with instructors helps develop a shared responsibility for teaching and learning that extends beyond the classroom (Cook-Sather, 2009).

Deciding which group to pursue involves considering what you want consultants to bring to the SGID (e.g., expertise in pedagogy, ability to collect authentic feedback from students). Experienced instructors will bring more pedagogical experience than students, but students, especially undergraduates, will connect with students more easily, likely resulting in more authentic conversations. Ensuring that SGID consultants are a good fit for the institutional culture is essential, especially because the consultants engage directly with both students and instructors. The campus must respect the SGID consultant and trust their ability to facilitate the SGID conversations and offer ideas to inform midcourse corrections that enhance learning. We emphasize the need for a robust training program, especially for student consultants, that empowers them to effectively engage in the SGID conversations. (See chapter 4 as well as following sections for more details on consultant training.)

Another way to expand the reach of the SGID program is to encourage departments, programs, or other areas of the institution to offer the SGID as an optional part of mentoring programs or feedback methods used to support reflective teaching practices for their faculty. Decentralizing SGID efforts brings the SGID closer to the instructor-to-instructor SGID experience we explored in chapter 3 and can be supported by the CTL through consultant training sessions. Although this type of SGID may never replace the service offered by centers, it can expand the reach of the program, while providing shared ownership of the SGID experience across the institution.

Enhancing SGID Consultant Training

In chapter 3 we reviewed the guiding principles consultants should embrace when engaging in the SGID conversations. These guiding principles in combination with the basic consultant training elements from chapter 4 provide a solid foundation for consultant training (Table 7.1). Enhancing consultant training requires iterative attention to these principles and training elements, ensuring that new and experienced consultants engage in conversations and observations that continually improve their facilitation skills. Moreover, developing additional, more advanced training elements for consultants can enhance the SGID experience by improving consultant confidence and their sense of belonging to the SGID team. Training sessions can be scheduled at the beginning of each term, especially for new SGID consultants, or throughout the term. Longer sessions (2–3 hours) at the beginning of the term provide time for more in-depth activities, whereas shorter sessions (45–60 minutes) during the term can support reflective activities. It is also beneficial to meet at the end of the term to debrief with consultants about their experiences and things they would find useful in future training sessions. In the following, we examine ways to integrate case studies, develop instructional consultation skills, and offer reflection activities that support consultation development.

SGID Case Studies

Doing SGIDs is one of the best ways to improve and grow as an SGID consultant. Every SGID is a unique experience, offering insights on how the SGID conversations unfold, the issues expressed by the students, and the ways instructors respond to the feedback. Some SGIDs inspire new ways of viewing class discussions or assignments. Other SGIDs reveal deep divisions in the student feedback, showing how students in the same course can view the learning environment in radically different ways. And some SGIDs are puzzling in that the student feedback seems at odds with the ways the instructor views elements of the course. Analysis and conversations about SGID case studies are an excellent way to help novice consultants navigate the uneven waters of the SGID conversation with the students and instructors. Rather than waiting for new consultants to experience a range of different SGIDs, case studies provide consultants with opportunities to engage with situations that reflect actual SGID experiences.

The SGID team at James Madison University developed cases representing common SGID scenarios to provide the consulting team with role-playing opportunities (Appendix E). Each term, new and experienced SGID consultants gathered to engage in conversations and role-play about each case. The cases were designed to give consultants training dealing with different kinds of instructors—apathetic instructors (Annabella), instructors with

TABLE 7.1
SGID Consultant Training Elements

Guiding Principles	• Be impartial. • Foster learning-centered conversations. • Explore meaningful course corrections.
Basic Training Elements	• Experience the SGID in one of their courses. • Watch a trained consultant run an SGID (including in-class conversation and faculty consultation). • Have a trained consultant observe the new consultant run an SGID. • Receive feedback on their SGID facilitation skills.
Advanced Training Elements	• Engage in SGID case study analysis. • Develop instructional consultation skills. • Incorporate reflection activities.

habits the students found distracting (Paul), instructors with challenging personalities (Ricki), and instructors nervous about what the students might say about them (Norm). These cases include the SGID results from the student session along with a bit of backstory. A few of the cases include the learner-centered SGID questions, which ask students to reflect on their role in the learning process. Depending upon the needs of the consultants, training sessions with these cases could involve the development of summaries or themes from the student feedback, development of strategies to approach the conversation with the instructor, and/or role-playing experiences that allow consultants to refine ways they approach different instructors and different kinds of SGID results. Case study training sessions using the details provided in Appendix E can result in "Ah-ha" moments for both new and returning consultants, while also building community within the team. At the end of the day, you can opt to use results from SGIDs at your institution rather than the results represented by the cases we provide, but these cases can help you get started with consultant training as you get your program off the ground.

Instructional Consultation Skills

SGID consultants engage both students and faculty in conversations about teaching and learning. In effect, SGID consultants are instructional consultants, striving to improve courses and enhance student learning. Effective instructional consultants bring their knowledge and expertise in teaching to the consultation by helping students and faculty unpack some of the more complex problems of teaching and learning (Fink & Sorenson, 2012). Often the SGID feedback points to obvious midcourse corrections. Students may report that they do not go to office hours because many of them have another class during the times offered by their instructor. The solution to this is to encourage the instructor to change their office hour schedule to accommodate more students. Other types of feedback often do not lead to simple solutions. For example, students might indicate that they do not understand the instructor's expectations for grading group projects. To better understand how to address this feedback, the consultant should ask the students about the information provided by their instructor and why they are finding it difficult to understand the expectations. The consultant should also inquire about the kind of feedback they get from the instructor and how they use this feedback. When the consultant debriefs with the instructor about this issue, the consultant should let the instructor explain their views on grading, outlining expectations and providing feedback. If the consultant is a knowledgeable instructional consultant, they would ask about the use of rubrics and offer to review the rubric during the consultation. The consultant might also offer suggestions regarding best practices in providing students with constructive feedback on their work. Novice consultants may or may not have experience with rubrics or may know little about rubric development and the best ways to use them to give students feedback. Thus, to improve the skills of SGID consultants, consultant training should include opportunities to enhance conceptual knowledge about teaching.

One method to enhance the conceptual knowledge consultants have about teaching is to adopt a common reading experience for the SGID consultant team. Asking consultants to read one or two books about teaching and then engaging them in conversations about these books offers opportunities to explore new ways of teaching. For example, *Small Teaching: Everyday Lessons From the Science of Learning* by James Lang (2016) offers insights on how to integrate the science of learning with activities that instructors can use to engage students in learning activities that support issues raised by the SGID. Alternatively, books such as *Making Learning-Centered Teaching Work: Practical Strategies for Implementation* by Phyllis Blumberg (2019) offer insights on the ways instructors can implement strategies to align with the aspirational aspects of the learner-centered teaching tenets. Additionally, these conversations inspired by a common reading can be directly applied to case study analysis, as described previously, where consultants can directly apply ideas from the texts to the SGID context. Consultants can also examine the SGID experience through the lens of pedagogical frameworks or their own teaching philosophies. Consultants can share insights from their own experiences on how aspects of their teaching philosophy guide their pedagogical decisions and practices. Through sharing experiences about their pedagogical design processes, consultants expand their conceptual understanding of teaching, especially in ways that challenge them to explore pedagogical issues and challenges in disciplines other than their own.

Reflection Activities

Professional growth of SGID consultants should encourage self-reflection activities that explore the stages of instructional consultant development and other consulting frameworks to inform their ongoing development as SGID consultants. Engaging SGID consultants in training sessions or discussions that explore the novice to expert developmental stages of instructional consultations can positively impact their skills. Wright et al. (2015) developed a modified version of the Tiberius et al. (1997) developmental stages model to analyze the development of graduate student consultants. The modified version of the developmental stages model outlines three stages of consultant expertise—novice/advanced beginner, competent/proficient, and expert

TABLE 7.2

Instructional Consultant Development Models and Frameworks

Model or Framework	Elements

Consultant expertise model (Wright et al., 2015, modified from Tiberius et al., 1997)	• Novice/advanced consultants
	  ○ follow a specific list of questions/procedures during the consultation.
	  ○ provide limited insights into possible solutions to problems.
	• Competent/proficient consultants
	  ○ identify problems or issues.
	  ○ offer some ideas on how to address these challenges.
	• Expert consultants
	  ○ easily identify problems that impact learning.
	  ○ engage instructor with variety of ideas to address the issues.

Consultation typologies (Brinko, 1997)	• Confrontational—the devil's advocate • Prescription—the solver of problems • Affiliative—the counselor • Product—the expert • Collaborative—the facilitator

Coaching framework (Little & Palmer, 2012)	• Deep listening
	  ○ discern needs, attitudes, motivation, and emotions of instructor
	  ○ consultant must reside in the moment, focus intently on the instructor, and listen nonjudgmentally
	• Asking powerful questions
	  ○ gather information
	  ○ organize thoughts
	  ○ clarify problems
	  ○ discover novel possibilities
	  ○ unlock creativity
	• Prompting action
	  ○ evoke a sense of purpose
	  ○ encourage risk-taking
	  ○ transform ideas into concrete strategies
	  ○ define goals
	  ○ focus thinking

(Wright et al., 2015). Each stage of development is aligned with how experience level influences the ways consultants identify and attempt to resolve classroom situations or problems (Table 7.2).

SGID training can also include opportunities for consultants to reflect on the consulting typologies developed by Brinko (1997). The consulting typologies—confrontational, prescription, affiliative, product, and collaborative—provide insights on the different approaches consultants use to interact with instructors and students during the SGID. Briefly, these typologies describe common approaches that consultants can use when engaging in the SGID conversations with students and instructors. The confrontational approach involves the consultant playing devil's advocate, encouraging the examination of ideas in ways that reveal logistical issues or other barriers that might impact implementation. The prescriptive approach is where the SGID consultant offers solutions to teaching and learning issues raised by the students and instructors. In our experiences, it is best for the consultant to avoid this approach, given our belief that the SGID consult should remain impartial. The affiliative approach is more in line with the tenets of the SGID, where the consultant acts as a counselor, challenging students and instructors to view feedback from the lens of the teaching and learning environment of the course. This approach is somewhat similar to both the product and collaborative approaches, both of which encourage the SGID consultant to use their expertise as instructors or students to collaboratively explore effective solutions to feedback items revealed during the SGID. Engaging SGID consultants in discussions or asking them to complete surveys that examine their consulting preferences reveal that consultants use a variety of approaches (Wright et al., 2015). These activities also highlight that there is no one right approach to engaging with the students and instructors in the SGID and that some consultants adjust their approach depending on the circumstances.

The coaching framework is another important framework CTLs can use to engage SGID consultants in reflective activities to develop deep listening skills, the ability to ask powerful questions, and strategies to encourage prompt action (Little & Palmer, 2012). Although this framework applies to all instructional consulting experiences, we feel it supports the SGID by highlighting and improving essential consulting skills. Initially, consultants can reflect the various consulting roles included in this framework and how they align with the SGID (e.g., data collector, facilitator, counselor). Consultants can also engage in activities developed by Little and Palmer (2012) to enhance deep listening skills, expand the use of powerful questions, and reflect on ways to encourage prompt action that embraces the SGID feedback.

Sidebar: The consultant mindsets and practices outlined in Table 7.2 have been instrumental to SGID consultant development in our center at Grand Valley State University. The consultant expertise model has helped us frame progress over time, assuring new consultants that they are not expected to have all of the answers right away, and also to help more experienced consultants reflect on their own journeys. In related staff SGID training sessions, the Brinko typologies allow us to frame expectations in approaching SGID consultations as collaborative, wherein the consultant partners with the instructor to take in the student feedback and plan a way forward in terms of responding to students and possibly also modifying teaching practices. The typologies also help us have SGID reflection conversations each semester, checking in to make sure that we each aren't straying too far into modes of problem-solving, counseling, or challenging instructors. I have also used the Brinko typologies and the coaching framework elements to help describe the SGID to instructors and academic administrators. Whether in describing what an instructional consultant will and will not do as part of an SGID or clarifying the difference between an SGID and an evaluative peer observation, being able to lean on these models has helped us articulate intent and expectations.—Christine M. Rener

Improving Midcourse Corrections

Making the most of the SGID results requires all members of the village—the SGID consultant, faculty, and students—to focus on midcourse corrections that improve learning. When we surveyed and interviewed educational developers about SGID success stories, many of the respondents indicated that the SGID succeeded in providing confidential, formative feedback to faculty that allowed them to develop actionable midcourse corrections to their courses. These midcourse corrections often led to self-reported lasting improvements in teaching and also to improved teaching reviews. They also indicated that because the rich and actionable feedback from the SGID comes from neutral facilitators (the SGID consultants), instructors valued and even welcomed the feedback. Respondents championed the ways that students were directly impacted by the SGID, often commenting about the SGID in course evaluations, sharing that they felt heard and had a sense that the instructor cared enough about them to use class time for this important program. Thus, the SGID succeeds in developing reflective teaching practices, where students see feedback enacted as their instructors embrace feedback and implement course corrections that improve the teaching and learning experience.

There are ways to improve the kinds of course corrections instructors and students make as a result of the SGID. One strategy is to engage in strategic planning conversations that examine each element of the SGID and explore changes to the process that could improve the quality of the feedback, the SGID conversations, and the impact of the SGID on instructors and students (Figure 7.1). For example, close analysis of how the consultant frames the SGID prior to SGID Conversation 1 or ways to include more student voices in Conversation 3 could lead to enhanced student understanding of their role in the SGID and a more representative set of results from the student conversation. This type of analysis resulted in the development of the learner-centered questions that Carol's team started using, which ultimately led to positive changes in student behaviors as a result of the SGID (Hurney et al., 2014). Strategic conversations about the SGID process could reveal better ways to connect consultants with instructors, introduce the SGID to students, create more inclusive environments to collect student feedback, and more.

There is no list of magical midsemester course corrections that address feedback provided during SGIDs. And there is no formula for helping instructors determine which course corrections will be the best options for them and their students. However, because many common themes emerge across SGIDs semester after semester, centers and instructors can get a bit of a head start through dissecting some of the more complex issues. Analyzing the aggregate SGID results from previous semesters can provide insights into the most common issues raised, offering a window where instructors

Figure 7.1. Overall SGID process.

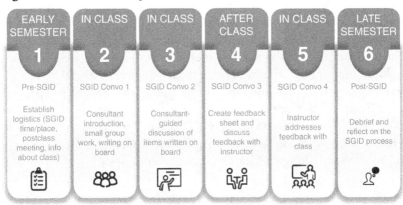

and centers can examine the literature on these issues. This head start can involve the curation and dissemination of resources, the development of programs that target common themes in the SGID results, and discussion of strategies that can be implemented at the beginning of the term to mitigate the ways these issues impact learning.

Sidebar: One of the most common issues raised during the SGID at Colby College is about the role of office hours. Students indicate that office hours help learning and that they should go to office hours more often. Further conversation during the SGID reveals that many students, especially first-generation students, don't really understand the purpose of office hours or are intimidated by them. When instructors hear this feedback, they are often surprised, because they feel that their office hours are welcoming places for all students. Knowing that this is a common issue students experience across disciplines resulted in the CTL offering sessions about office hours, discussing this issue with faculty in other settings, and implementing a pedagogical partner program where students work with faculty to make all aspects of their courses more inclusive, including office hours.—Carol A. Hurney

---

Creating Spaces for Dialogue About the SGID

Talking about the SGID matters. Talking about how the SGID impacts learning matters more. And getting students and faculty to talk about how the SGID changes learning matters most. The biggest ripple effect that emanates from an SGID program is the impact on the campus dialogue about teaching and learning. Starting from the first SGID conversations where the students talk with each other about teaching and learning to the conversations that happen after the SGID, when instructors talk with other instructors within and across disciplines, the SGID fosters a sense of trust in the students by valuing their voices through the SGID process. More importantly, the SGID conversations strengthen relationships between faculty and their students, foregrounding the student perspective and clarifying misconceptions of both faculty and students about what learning looks like in a course. The SGID opens up a space to talk about the research on teaching and learning—with students, colleagues, and members of the teaching and learning centers on campus.

Craig (2007) used the SGID to seed conversations about developing supportive and formative teaching evaluation culture within the Department of Computer Science at the University of Toronto. Based on their collective realization that the end of the semester course evaluations provided little, if any, constructive comments from their students, they wanted to implement a more direct method of collecting student feedback. Rather than turn their efforts toward developing a peer review process, they turned to the SGID. Over the course of 3 years over 50% of the faculty voluntarily signed up to have an SGID for at least one of their courses. Results from their analysis of the SGID program suggest that the SGID improved teaching quality and strengthened the value that both faculty and administrators put on teaching.

Finally, the SGID provides a centering experience, through a range of conversations that support metacognitive reflection about how we think about the teaching and learning endeavor. In fact, the best conversations about the SGID come when SGID consultants, instructors, and students gather in formal and informal spaces to talk about what they learned from their SGID experience. Hopefully, these conversations take place when the instructors engage their students in the last SGID conversation, where the instructor responds to the student feedback about learning issues. But these conversations can also take place when instructors and students gather, at the end of the term, in focus groups or other settings, to explore the ripple effects of the SGID. In effect these conversations are ways of using the SGID to reflect on the SGID. Yes, SGIDing the SGID is a thing (and a mouthful) and can be one of the best ways to enhance the SGID experience. Asking three simple questions—*What helped your understanding of learning in the SGID? What hindered your understanding of learning in the SGID? What suggestions do you have to improve the ways the SGID impacted your understanding of learning?*—elevates the SGID and provides insights on how this simple program can impact the classroom experience, student learning, and the campus academic culture.

8

ENGAGING IN SGID RESEARCH

A few years ago I served as a consulting editor for the SoTL journal Teaching of Psychology. *In that role, I reviewed dozens of manuscripts. Some of them were terrific research examples: rigorous, insightful, and directly applicable to classroom outcomes. But unfortunately, many others—perhaps most—were not. These less stellar submissions were often missing something important—a control variable not included in the analysis, an unexamined confounding variable, or a crucial design flaw. As I'd come to find out, at least when compared to many other fields of scholarship, SoTL is in a nascent form, just beginning to build up its methodologies and evidence base.*

In responding to these manuscripts, I found myself making three primary suggestions to authors, which are the same suggestions I'd make to future SGID researchers. First, make it matter. *Make sure that the research question you're hoping to answer is one of import to a relevant audience. Second,* make it new. *Unless your work fits into the category of a direct replication attempt, make sure that it addresses a new question, or one that extends previous work in an interesting way. Third,* make it better. *Figure out the methodology that's appropriate to answer your question, then use it. Or if your first study on a topic is a hypothesis-generating endeavor, then call it a pilot study and build on it with a more rigorous second study.*

I've provided this feedback frequently because student learning is important. To me, it is at least as important as many of the variables we may examine in our other research pursuits. And if we do not do this type of research right, we are letting our students down. I've been doing psychological research for a long time, and a failed study in my disciplinary work is a disappointment. But they're not nearly as big of a disappointment as the failed studies I've done in the field of SoTL. Those are not just failures for me but failures for a group of students as well. Let's work hard to get firm answers to our questions about what happens in our courses. Our lives and our students' lives will be all the richer for it.

—Jordan D. Troisi

For each of us authors, this is the first book we have authored. And like most of us feel with new experiences, we were a little intimidated by it. We had our doubts; we had our ups and downs. But a couple of things kept us moving forward. We knew the SGID was worth holding up for the world to see. We knew the SGID should be put forward so we could give classes the formative feedback they deserved—to ask: *What is happening in here, and what else could there be?*

We knew from our experiences that SGID can prompt the profound reanalysis that our courses so often deserve. But a lot of this "knowing" was all in our heads—a hunch, a belief, a feeling. These things are hard to measure. Fortunately, though, hard to measure doesn't mean impossible to measure.

We are indebted to our many colleagues in the last 30–40 years who have started to mount scholarly evidence, piece by piece, of the importance and efficacy of SGID. There are many of these colleagues, but we'd submit that there are not enough, or maybe that their voices haven't been heard widely enough. Many of those we surveyed and interviewed while writing this book wanted to be able to draw from an authoritative source to convince their stakeholders of the value of SGID, to be able to say, "Here is why we dedicate so much time and effort to make SGIDs happen." We hope that this book will serve as at least a part of that authoritative evidence.

But even with the body of mostly favorable evidence for SGID that exists already, there is still so much yet to be discovered. This is how research goes: You answer one question and it leads you to the next question, and the next, and the next. Will a finding cut across institutions of different sizes, contexts, cultures, and approaches? Who are the many parties affected by SGID processes, and how lasting are those effects? What more do we want to know about SGID right now, and what more will we want to know after we have answered that next question, and the next, and the next?

Some might view research in higher education as an act of frivolity, a method through which those of us in the ivory tower, a class of individuals who mostly have immense privilege, examine their ultra specific, idiosyncratic musings. But we'd make a different argument, at least when it comes to research about pedagogy and research on SGID. To us, these topics are high stakes. How many students are in our instructors' classes every semester? How many hours do our instructors spend with our students each semester? How many interactions do they have with them, all in the service of helping students learn effectively? How might we check in, partway through the semester, to take stock and think about the most effective pathway forward?

To not research—to not seek a better understanding about the classroom environment—seems like a grave mistake.

This is how we think about research on SGID. It matters, it matters greatly, and it matters to so many. When we conduct effective research, we know more. When we fail to do so, we fail to realize the opportunities we have to help the many important people on our campuses: our students and our instructors who help them learn. We hold this lesson close to our hearts, and we hope you will too, as you help us consider the many questions still worth answering about SGID.

In some ways, this chapter is quite a bit different from our other chapters. In our other chapters, we mostly look inward at SGID: How can SGIDs be conducted, what impact have they had on a department or campus, and how can an SGID program get started on a campus? In this chapter we take a different approach. We take our knowledge and understandings about the SGID, place ourselves right in the middle of it, then look outward into the distance and ask ourselves: *What else could there be?* To research a topic requires this kind of adventuresome spirit, a willingness to journey out into the unknown. It also requires some humility in taking in the information we might find. If we are to research a topic like SGID, we must take that concept and generalize it to other places and populations. We cannot assume that there is only one right way forward; there might be a handful of ways, all a little different from one another, that all align on the same core principles. We must figure out, even with little tweaks on this campus or that campus, what core features of SGID ring true wherever the process occurs. Although SGIDs are often examined with an inward lens (*How can we make this program more effective on our campus?*), for research the outward lens is required (*How can we tell a story about SGID that would make sense just about everywhere?*).

We hope you are thinking about these questions, asking these questions, and seeking answers to them. Because there is much we still need to know. Like a fair amount of research areas in SoTL and the Scholarship of Educational Development, research on SGID is just scratching the surface of its potential. As we reported in other chapters, there are a handful of data-driven studies that attest to SGID's value, but there is much more we do not yet know. From our point of view, this makes it an exciting time for research on SGID. And we think this is an important endeavor, too. The questions and answers that research uncovers will have ripple effects on countless instructors and their students.

Taken in its totality, there is a firm base of research that elucidates how students and instructors feel about SGID. Compared to many other classroom interventions, both students and faculty report liking the SGID process (e.g., Abbott et al., 1990; Clark & Redmond, 1982; Craig, 2007; Crow et al., 2008; Finelli et al., 2008; Hurney et al., 2014; Sherry et al., 1998; Wulff et al., 1985). Faculty also report making changes based on the presence of SGIDs in their courses (e.g., Craig, 2007; Diamond, 2004; Finelli et al., 2008). Some researchers have also found that SGID seems to have a positive impact on instructors' end-of-semester course evaluations (e.g., Finelli et al., 2008; Wulff et al., 1985). Those who are interested in embracing SGID on their campuses should, rightly so, feel comfortable that they are engaging in a practice that will meet with support from key constituencies.

But these findings are just the tip of the iceberg. There is much more to know about the impact of SGID, and we have every confidence that more research on it will bring additional supportive evidence of its efficacy. Drawing from an existing framework for high-quality research on SoTL, in this chapter we will suggest methodologically strong approaches that will cement SGID as a best practice in educational development, and also pinpoint gaps in SGID research topics that are ripe for the picking.

Improving the SGID Research Base

In recent years, a number of authors have more thoroughly and clearly articulated high-quality standards for research on teaching and learning (e.g., Wilson-Doenges & Gurung, 2013). Unlike early work in SoTL, in which many publications were primarily opportunities to share teaching approaches, modern SoTL is designed to uphold and demonstrate rigorous, replicable research practices. Drawn from SoTL in the field of psychology, one approach to evaluating the quality of existing research involves the integration of "gold standard" approaches (Wilson-Doenges et al., 2016). What's more, these gold standard approaches, shown in Table 8.1, can also suggest pathways for new research based on the body of research evidence that already exists related to SGIDs. In the following sections, we will sample from this framework and highlight some areas where research on SGIDs may embrace these gold standards, and in turn, produce more powerful and persuasive evidence of efficacy. (Of course, many frameworks for desirable research practices could be applied to understanding the impact of SGIDs. The gold standards approach is one model that stands out as fairly comprehensive and relevant, but it is by no means the definitive approach.)

Theory-Based

Grounding research in existing theoretical examinations has many benefits. Here are three. First, doing so provides a robust evidence base through which

TABLE 8.1
Gold Standards for SoTL

- theory-based
- longitudinal designs that track responses over time, with good response rates and appropriate analysis techniques
- experimental design that includes random assignment and double-blind procedures
- large sample sizes and established power of statistical tests
- use of advanced and multivariate statistical analyses
- samples taken from more than one institution with some diversity
- high standard of ethics
- mixed-method approaches—using both qualitative and quantitative data analyzed appropriately

researchers can formulate arguments and hypotheses. Second, using previous established methods and variables ensures reasonable levels of reliability and validity in measurement tools. Third, rooting research questions in a theoretical base allows for natural integration of current findings within a previous body of work.

Most of the existing research on SGID has not drawn from established theoretical models in SoTL that might explain its effectiveness, at least not directly. Perhaps somewhat surprisingly, some of the earliest research on SGID was formulated with an existing theoretical base: working on the assumption that involvement in SGIDs procedures would be associated with student motivation (e.g., Clark & Redmond, 1982; Redmond, 1982). But little research since then has directly tied SGID to this or other theoretical constructs that are well rooted in effective course design and pedagogical practice (e.g., learner-centered teaching, active learning, inclusive teaching).

Sticking first to questions associated with motivation, we think there is much more yet to be examined when it comes to how SGIDs may influence motivation, a concept with a rich theoretical background in psychology (e.g., Ryan & Deci, 2000, 2017), as well as a burgeoning base of research in educational development (e.g., the POD 2017 Robert J. Menges Award for Outstanding Research in Educational Development was awarded to a project examining teaching motivations). One macro theory for understanding human motivation is self-determination theory (Chen et al., 2015; Deci & Ryan, 2000; Sheldon & Gunz, 2009), which assumes that humans are motivated to fulfill needs for autonomy (i.e., feelings of control over one's life outcomes), relatedness or belonging (i.e., feelings of interpersonal connection), and competence (i.e., feelings of self-efficacy at tasks; Deci & Ryan, 2000). Greater satisfaction of these needs leads to greater feelings of intrinsic motivation in the classroom. Looking only from the lens of self-determination theory, here are some research questions that come to mind for us:

- Given that SGIDs provide an opportunity for students to express factors associated with their courses that they feel either are or are not helping their learning, do courses that use an SGID increase students' feelings of autonomy and intrinsic motivation?
- Given the types of connection fostered by SGIDs—student to student and student to professor—do SGIDs impact students' feelings of belonging? Do they also increase feelings of belonging for instructors as well?
- Do instructors feel an increase in their levels of competence associated with their teaching after receiving feedback and implementing corrections in their courses based on student feedback from SGIDs?

Moving closer to pedagogical theory, there is a long-standing tradition of examining instructor–student rapport and its impact on classroom-related outcomes (Legg & Wilson, 2009; Ryan et al., 2011; Wilson & Ryan, 2013). Newer research on rapport also demonstrates that students' feelings of rapport with their instructors have favorable downstream effects on their grades (Lammers et al., 2017). Drawing from this body of evidence, here are two research questions that come to mind:

- Do SGIDs have a direct impact on established measures of student–professor rapport?
- Does an increase in student–professor rapport account for the potential increase in student performance outcomes after an SGID has occurred?

Finally, researchers have designed some measures intended to describe effective, ideal, or aspirational teaching practices. For example, Keeley et al. (2006, 2010, 2016) have gathered a rich collection of student and instructor perspectives on excellent teaching and developed a measure known as the Teacher Behavior Checklist that students can complete about their instructor. Additionally, Boysen et al. (2015) and Richmond et al. (2016) have more recently elucidated a set of aspirational approaches to teaching, collected via self-report questionnaire, that are relatively easy to implement for teachers with any degree of experience. As educational developers, from our point of view, this leads to a couple of natural research questions:

- Do instructors who regularly engage in SGIDs meet more criteria for teaching excellence?
- Does engaging in SGIDs move instructors closer to ideal teaching practices, or teaching excellence (either as self-reported, observed, or rated by students)?

Longitudinal Designs That Track Responses Over Time, With Good Response Rates

The ability to examine outcomes over some time course and, ideally, over many different time periods is highly desirable in SoTL and the Scholarship of Educational Development. Doing so allows researchers to state what has changed, when it has changed, and how long the change lasted. If we assume that student learning, for example, is something that will impact students' lives after our courses, or after they have completed college, then we are already working on the implicit assumption that outcomes that unfold over time should be of interest to us as educators. Of course, collecting data on students over time (either within a course or after a course has ended) is often a difficult process. But that is precisely what makes such data so valuable. And with SGIDs being a midcourse correction—an intervention introduced about halfway through the semester—they seem like a topic made for the kind of analysis that might examine outcomes at multiple points in time.

There have been a modest number of studies conducted on SGIDs, and some include a substantial number of classes, instructors, and consultants (see, e.g., Finelli et al., 2008; Hurney et al., 2014). However, to our knowledge, very few of these studies have come close to examining true longitudinal outcomes. Furthermore, our survey data indicate that many of the variables that might appropriately be assessed over time (e.g., student learning, faculty retention, impact on consultants) are not a part of SGID assessment processes in place at institutions that conduct SGID. Some existing studies have compared feedback provided at the midpoint of the semester—around the time of the SGID—with end-of-course feedback, but these types of feedback about teaching are not identical and only give us part of the story. To us, what appears to be missing are studies that examine one variable, or multiple variables, in an identical fashion at multiple time periods, as in the following examples:

- How does having an SGID influence students' impressions of their instructor right after it occurs, and then weekly throughout the remainder of the semester?

- Or, perhaps a bit more elaborate than the first idea, what are students' impressions of an instructor like during the first week of the semester, right after the SGID, and during the last week of the semester?
- How do instructors feel about their courses before, immediately after, and long after conducting an SGID?

Given that SGIDs are often administered through CTLs, students may encounter many of them during their time in college, or a few, or none at all. This leads us to wonder:

- Are there cumulative effects related to student outcomes based on how many SGID procedures they've experienced?

Perhaps students who have engaged in many SGID procedures would think about education in a fundamentally different way than most other students—as a process in which students and faculty engage in a feedback loop, with frequent adjustments to pedagogical practices based on that feedback. The same type of research inquiry could target departments as well, with research questions such as the following:

- If certain departments engage in many SGIDs (versus those who engage in few, or none at all), might this be related to how students perceive the departments in which they take their courses?

Perhaps departments that engage in a high proportion of a university's SGID procedures are perceived as ones with a healthy culture of teaching, a distinct dedication to their students, or a growth mindset related to pedagogy.

SGID data collection on instructors, like students, has not often examined outcomes in a longitudinal way. But it would be fruitful to do so. Some instructors have never been part of an SGID, some have been part of one or a few, and some have been part of many. Is it possible that these individuals may think about teaching in general, or even teaching a particular course, differently from one another? How might involvement in SGIDs influence instructors' appreciation of pedagogy (Hurney et al., 2020), the development of their learning goals for their courses, or the time it takes them to develop new courses? Perhaps participating in multiple SGIDs allows instructors—through receiving regular feedback from students and trained consultants—to develop a clearer vision of their priorities for learning outcomes in their courses. These are outcomes that could be tracked over a more substantial time course as well, such as longitudinal changes in teaching practices based on instructor career stage. The data will tell if these outcomes, or some other meaningful ones, will emerge.

Experimental Design That Includes Random Assignment and Double-Blind Procedures

Experimental designs require manipulation of an independent variable, random assignment of participants to different conditions of that independent variable, and control over other confounding variables. The benefit of experimental designs is that they allow the researchers to assert causal claims about the relationships between the variables under examination.

Certainly, true experimental designs are a high bar to set for most educational research. Often, at the very least, it is difficult to randomly assign participants to different experimental conditions. Nevertheless, true double-blind experiments are possible, and they allow researchers to achieve high degrees of certainty in the effectiveness of a pedagogical procedure. For example, Legg and Wilson (2009) used a double-blind experimental approach to examine how sending a welcome email before a course begins can build rapport and bolster student motivation and course attitudes. In their study, prior to the beginning of the course, a colleague of the instructor sent a welcome email to a random selection of half of the students. The instructor continued with the course as she normally would, not knowing which of the students received the welcome email (being "blind" to which students were in which group). The results revealed that students who received the welcome email reported more favorable SETs related to the course and the instructor, particularly in the early class periods. Creative study designs such as this one can be used to generate strong evidence for pedagogical approaches.

Much of the past research on SGIDs has relied on less rigorous research approaches, including anecdotal reports or nonexperimental designs. This is reasonable in the early, exploratory stages of research on a topic, and this pattern mirrors the pattern of the development of SoTL research areas. But some previous work on SGIDs has moved past this point and utilized experimental manipulations, which we commend when it is possible. For example, Hurney et al. (2014) randomly assigned instructors at a large institution into conditions in which their SGID was conducted using either more traditional response questions on student feedback sheets or learner-centered response questions. Results revealed that students asked to reflect on their own involvement in the learning process (i.e., the learner-centered SGID) showed statistically significant increases in aspects of their learning controlled by themselves (i.e., course preparation, interactions with classmates). Another study (Abbott et al., 1990), with an elaborate 2 × 2 × 2 design, experimentally manipulated the type of feedback requested by students (SGID vs. SETs), the timing of this feedback (4th week of a 10-week quarter vs. 9th week of a 10-week quarter), and duration of the instructor reaction procedures (extended vs. limited). Results revealed, among other findings, that students were more satisfied with the SGID process than with the SETs.

Although extremely rigorous designs are not possible in all circumstances, for the sake of solidifying the evidence base demonstrating that SGID is an effective practice, we recommend researchers move toward more experimental approaches. This could include random assignment of instructors, students, or consultants to different conditions of a manipulated variable. It could also include statistical control over confounding variables, and providing stringent comparison groups that allow for assertions that the interventions produce effects above and beyond doing nothing at all, or engaging in a standard existing practice.

Here's a hypothetical example: Let's say that staff members at a CTL were interested in finding out if SGIDs that occurred at the beginning of the class period or at the end of class had a greater impact on the number of comments students made during the SGID. Of course, it would be impossible to render the consultant blind to which type of SGID they were conducting (otherwise they would arrive at the wrong time!), but the consultants could be randomly assigned to conduct some of their SGIDs at the beginning of the class and some at the end (and SGIDs in different departments, programs, and so on could also be randomly assigned to one of these two conditions). Then, after all the data were collected, researchers could code and examine whether having the SGID process at the beginning or the end of class produced more comments from students.

Advanced and Multivariate Statistical Analyses (When Appropriate)

An area that strikes as one where researchers could improve their approaches to examining SGIDs would be in the selection and use of established self-report questionnaires that have been validated by previous research. Self-report questionnaires are a mainstay of classroom research, and they can measure everything from individual differences between people (e.g., feelings of self-efficacy) to personality constructs (e.g., conscientiousness) to the consequences of manipulated or predictive variables (e.g., the effects on student feelings of autonomy after a teacher intervention). However, too often, SGID researchers have not used complete questionnaires in their analyses of data, and have instead only used portions of an established questionnaire and computed mean values based on that portion of the items. Doing so is against recommendations that might be considered "best practices." This methodological approach can weaken the overall statistical test the researchers wish to conduct. It also ignores efforts to establish validity and reliability of that questionnaire from previous research (calling into question the real meaning of any findings that might emerge). And perhaps most problematic, this process can also suggest duplicity in research approaches (i.e., "fishing" for the findings that match one's hypothesis and throwing out the findings that do not). For these reasons, when possible, we urge researchers to select questionnaires that they think will meaningfully represent the variables of interest to them, seek out the previous work that validates those questionnaires, and report the findings of the entire questionnaire.

Another area in which we see room for improvement in research on SGIDs is through the use of appropriate statistical controls in data analysis (e.g., to limit the effect of confounding variables, to rule out alternative explanations). When experiments are well designed, their methodology provides control over extraneous variables. Random assignment can ensure, for example, that a similar gender breakdown will occur across experimental conditions. But sometimes it is not always possible to methodologically control for potential intervening variables. To remedy this, these variables could be measured, then statistically controlled for in the data analysis phase.

Here's an example. Say a group of researchers are curious if students' grades in a course affect how much they perceive having an SGID to be valuable. Of course, researchers cannot ethically manipulate students' grades in a course, so the best thing they can do is measure students' grades and take this into account when conducting statistical tests. They can gather this information by either asking students their grades during the research procedure or procuring those grades from the office on campus that houses them. Then, students' grades can be entered as a control variable or covariate in other statistical tests.

To provide another example, it seems reasonable to us to assume that the degree to which students respond in socially desirable ways may impact the eventual outcomes of SGID procedures. For example, students' responses to SGIDs may reflect that they will change their study habits for the remainder of their time in a course, but such responding is socially desirable in educational settings, and it may not in fact be true. To help tease apart how students really feel or what they really believe will occur, researchers could examine and treat as a covariate participants' tendency to respond to questionnaires in socially desirable ways. There are many tools for measuring socially desirable responding, including simple self-report measures that participants can complete themselves (e.g., Crowne & Marlowe, 1960).

We acknowledge that, because those who may wish to research SGID may come from a variety of disciplinary backgrounds, topics associated with multivariate data analysis may be unfamiliar to many. But we think this fact highlights the possibility to develop valuable research collaborations. Perhaps there is someone not affiliated with your research team who has a background in statistics, psychology, or educational research who could help design or analyze studies on the topic. Perhaps there is someone on your campus who is skilled at examining open-ended discussions and may contribute to the SGID research endeavor. Or, as we will delve deeper into in the next section, perhaps there are interested collaborators at other institutions who have a firm background in the kind of methodological and data analytic techniques that will provide answers to the questions you have.

Samples Taken From More Than One Institution, With Some Diversity

As mentioned at the outset of this chapter, a scholarly approach can allow us to say something bigger about SGID as a process for providing midterm corrections in courses. To the extent that SGID researchers would like to establish that the SGIDs are a broadly effective practice, and not simply an artifact of how they are implemented on their campus, they should seek out collaborators at other institutions. This is referred to as generalizability: Do the findings from an intervention conducted at one institution mirror the effects of a similar intervention at another institution?

We understand that addressing this issue is often easier said than done. Doing so requires collaboration, often in long-term form, standardization of research procedures and tools (e.g., questionnaires), and frequent communication about the nature of a potential research study. But jumping through these hoops would help establish an important principle—that SGID is an impactful and valuable procedure—and not just one educational intervention that works at one institution because of the idiosyncrasies of that place or its procedures.

One of the benefits of this type of collaborative research approach is that it gets people talking about how they conduct SGID on their campuses, and how they might do so in a way that is similar or distinct from their colleagues. Indeed, we three authors of this book have found that although we shared some common ideas about how to conduct SGIDs, we also had some differences in how we went about the process (both small and large). And these conversations have enriched the practices on each of our campuses. More of these conversations across institutions could galvanize the process of SGID, and lead to more common language and thought about SGID.

Because research on SGID most often occurs within one institution or one department, we think there are many areas left to explore when looking across institutions. One that jumps out at us, coming from both liberal arts colleges and a large regional university, has to do with institution size. For example, at Colby College, with an enrollment of around 1,900 students, many students are familiar with the SGID process. They have seen it in many of their courses, they have seen it across departments, and because their classes tend to be smaller, they have seen it occur in mostly small classes. (Because the staffing of the CTL at Colby is smaller in size than the CTLs at many other institutions, if students have done an SGID in many of their courses, they have probably run into the same consultants as well.) Might the areas in which SGID could have an impact look different at larger institutions, with larger classes? The evidence remains to be seen, and cross-institutional research will provide it. Might SGID evidence different outcomes at institutions with a heavy proportion of online classes, or lower number of students of traditional college age, or even at universities outside North America? Perhaps. The research evidence that exists so far does not yet give us adequate answers to these questions.

SGID as a Research Tool

We're under the assumption that most people who are reading this book have a fair amount of research experience in one disciplinary area or another. Some may have an awful lot, and some may have less. But we'd venture a guess that all of us know what it means to engage in the research process: to see something occurring in the world, to wonder about it, and to begin an investigation of it. In our work conducting and researching SGIDs, something has struck us. We believe that SGIDs are not only a thing to be researched but they also might *be the research tool.* We've seen some examples of this in the published literature already (e.g., Diamond, 2004; Sit & Brudzinski, 2017). For example, at one institution, SGID was used as an approach to gather faculty attitudes about the value—or lack thereof—of SETs (Blash et al., 2018). At another institution, library staff and faculty used SGID to evaluate students' perceptions of open education resource (OER) textbooks (Bazeley et al., 2019).

Why might the SGID be effective as a research approach? To us, the SGID mirrors the type of open-ended data collection from which many research questions begin to blossom (see, e.g., Hutchinson & Stoeckle, 2020). In the early stages of a research endeavor, in some fields called *pilot research*, the goal is often to generate lots of ideas in a relatively freeform fashion. The way we often think about it, the early research stage is an exciting one, where lots of ideas get thrown into the hopper as potential topics of further inquiry and scrutiny. These early stages are not usually for testing hypotheses; they are more often used for generating hypotheses. This is exactly the type of "data collection" that occurs in virtually every SGID classroom session we have ever conducted. In some ways, the information collected from working with students in an SGID classroom session is the pilot data that tells the instructor how to make adaptations for the remainder of that course. For example, SGID responses can tell the instructor where students are having trouble with readings, what aspects of homework are helpful or not so helpful, or the pathways through which professor-to-student communication is most effective. This "pilot data" allows the instructor to make corrections for the remainder of the course.

The classroom is the most frequently used place for SGIDs as a research tool, but it's not the only place. If we think about the process of an SGID—a consultant works with a group of participants, collects their feedback, delivers that feedback to the group leader, and discusses pathways forward with the leader—it sounds like an effective problem-solving tool. And a few places where it could be used come to mind. How about in a large department with faculty members who are stalled or deadlocked in finding a pathway for the problem of the hour (enrollment pressures, morale, distribution of duties, or you name it)? For example, a handful of researchers have utilized SGID to assist academic departments in assessing their outcomes of interest, such as program goals or pedagogical approaches (Bartholomew et al., 2018; Gooder & Cantwell, 2017; Remington et al., 2015). Or how about in university executive committee meetings where teams have to make high-stakes decisions, but often fail to engage in the thorough brainstorming and examination of the ideas first? In these places, as in many others, the SGID process will likely prove useful.

Outcomes Not Yet Examined

As we've mentioned earlier in this chapter, we think one of the benefits of the "gold standards" framework that we've used as a set of guiding principles is that they provide some good suggestions for developing research questions on SGIDs. These research questions could take many forms, including many we haven't even imagined yet. But in our examination of both the practice and research base of SGIDs, we've bumped into many questions that we have imagined, and for which we want answers. We've listed some in the previous sections, but we've got even more. The following lists are just a few, loosely categorized into categories about students, instructors, consultants, and SGID results. Although it's sometimes difficult to limit the questions to just one of these categories.

Questions Mostly About Students

- Is there evidence that students learn more effectively, persist at difficult tasks longer, write better papers, spend more hours studying, or answer test questions better because of the experience of an SGID in their course?

- We are unaware of any research that has examined the post-SGID consultation debriefing between the instructor and students. We would love to have researchers record some of these conversations and examine them (what is included in them, how long they take, how students respond to them).

- At the core of learner-centered teaching is the idea that instructors and students work collaboratively to help students realize learning outcomes. Do students perceive teaching and learning to be more collaborative if they've been a part of one or more SGIDs? Do students who've experienced more SGIDs show more collaborative attitudes, and if so, is there a plateau after which the impact fails to produce more gains?

- Does being a part of SGIDs have any distinct impact on students who have goals to be teachers (e.g., at the K–12 level, at the collegiate level)? Is this some of the earliest and most impactful training in pedagogy for current students?

Questions Mostly About Instructors

- Does engaging in one or more SGIDs impact the degree to which instructors adopt learner-centered approaches? Does it impact their willingness to provide accommodations to students or creativity in how those accommodations are provided?

- Does involvement in SGIDs increase instructors' appreciation of pedagogy or sharpen their learning objectives? That is, does engaging in SGID help instructors see a wider array of teaching practices or clarify their priorities? And does this have downstream effects on transparency in working with students?

- Is the SGID an entry point for other services that a CTL might provide? Is the SGID uniquely persuasive in helping instructors see the value of CTLs and, thus, an indicator that they will be involved in other CTL programs?

- Does engaging in SGIDs influence course development (does it make the process shorter, clearer, easier)?

- Does the SGID open up individuals to more input about their teaching? Does it make them more amenable to visitors in their classroom, or does it allow them to have a more collaborative or collegial approach to their work?

Questions Mostly About Consultants and Consultations

We know of no research that has examined how being a part of the SGID process might be associated with outcomes for the consultants and the consultation with the instructor. This is probably because the research that has been conducted on SGIDs more often includes consultants as a part of the research team, rather than a research subject. Nevertheless, from our own practice, we certainly think engaging in SGID consultations has had an impact on our own teaching, and perceive this outcome to be worthy of investigation.

- We'd like to see some research examining the conversation between the SGID consultant and the instructor. Both basic and thorough information is needed here. How long do these consultations last, where do they occur, what topics of conversation come up, and how are "good news" and "bad news" approached?
- Based on how the consultation goes, how do students perceive the effectiveness of the SGID procedure? If instructors are more "defensive" about receiving the feedback and hesitant to make changes, do students feel frustrated by the lack of change?
- What are the ways in which engaging in SGIDs affects the teaching of the consultant? Many SGIDs are conducted by graduate students, or part-time or full-time faculty members. Do they learn new approaches to their own teaching, adding new tools to their teacher's toolkit?

Questions Mostly About SGID Results

We are also curious about at least a handful of questions for which we think SGIDs might provide some clues:

- Do SGID results change over time based on instructor involvement in educational development interventions? For example, do individuals who engage in course design institutes see changes to the types of feedback they receive when they have SGIDs done in their classes?
- Does the feedback provided on SGIDs offer insights for CTLs about areas for growth that could be addressed through select interventions?
- Do the results of SGIDs provide feedback on instructor engagement in specific university strategic planning priorities (e.g., community

engagement; project-based learning; and diversity, equity, and inclusion initiatives)? In some ways, might SGIDs be the assessment data for strategic planning initiatives?

Looking Back, Looking Forward

As we approach the closing of this chapter and this book, we are reminded of the parallels we see between SGID and the research process. Research is always looking both inward and outward, looking back and looking forward. We look back, seeing where our colleagues started this examination of SGIDs some 40 years ago, the ideas they had, the questions they developed, the examinations that may have faltered or worked along the way. But we also look forward. We take the stories and evidence from the past, and turn our heads to the horizons, wondering to ourselves, what else could there be? This question is valid for the many research projects that should and will be conducted on SGID: What else could there be? And this question, too, is emblematic of the true in-class SGID experience, where teachers, students, and SGID consultants work together, engage in conversation, and problem-solve, forever striving together to answer the question *What else could there be?* We hope you will keep this question near your heart as you pursue all endeavors in the college classroom.

CONCLUSION

Unwrapping the Promise of the SGID

By this point in the book, we hope to have convinced you that you can easily integrate the SGID into your courses or center program offerings. We also hope you feel empowered to enhance the impact of the SGID in your context. But some of you might still be wondering if doing the SGID is really worth it. We end with a few thoughts about the ways the SGID has impacted our teaching and educational development work.

Jordan's Reflection

Among our authors, I'm the newest one to the SGID game. But I have been teaching in higher education for over 10 years, and I've always been fond of midsemester feedback in my own courses. It makes sense for me: Why wait until the end of the semester to see "how things went," when instead you could check in part way to see how things are going and make corrections along the way? In fact, many years ago, before I had heard of the SGID, I did some SoTL research on an ongoing feedback approach that leverages the power of a volunteer group of students in a course called Student Management Teams (Troisi, 2014, 2015).

But now I've found a home in SGIDs, and I don't want to leave it. In my own courses, I'd never go without midsemester feedback, and SGIDs do everything I'd want in a midsemester feedback process. They not only gather student voices but they also encourage and empower students to dig deeper and understand how their classroom and their instructor works. They break down the rigid barriers in communication and hierarchy that often exist between students and instructors. They give instructors new perspectives on the course in question, whether it's the first time they've taught it, or 50th.

As an educational developer as well, a big part of my work is to help instructors improve the teaching and learning in their classrooms. Working with instructors on their teaching is a fairly straightforward task, through workshops, learning communities, course design institutes, and the like. But, strangely, it's pretty rare for educational developers to work with students directly in order to understand their learning experiences and suggest course alterations. My role in developing SGID programs has been the single thing that has most directly reconnected me and other instructors with student learning. It's where the rubber meets the road.

Carol's Reflection

I met the SGID in my first role as an educational developer at the University of Virginia (UVa). The teaching center at UVa offered this consultation service to instructors and graduate students across all disciplines. The SGID experience opened up a world of teaching and learning for me that changed my entire career. Walking into classrooms, where I was free to talk with students about teaching and learning, and then bringing that conversation into consultations with instructors, shined a spectacular light on the ways teaching can support and also hinder learning.

I was so moved by the power of the SGID to inform instruction and support the ways that instructors thought about teaching that I have started an SGID program at every institution I have worked at. At first, I created an informal SGID program with my faculty colleagues in the biology department of James Madison University (JMU). The success of this program led to the development of a university-wide SGID program within the emerging center for faculty development—and to the solidification of my career path as an educational developer. When applying for the director role of the faculty development center at JMU, I repeatedly proclaimed that if I could only offer one program to support teaching and learning at JMU, it would be the SGID program. And when I left JMU to become the founding director of the CTL at Colby College, I started the SGID program during my first semester on campus, for the very same reasons that I was so moved by my first SGID experiences at UVa.

The SGID keeps delivering on its promise to open up the world of teaching and learning to me and the faculty I work with. The SGID helps me better support the teaching and learning culture at my institution by connecting me with both faculty and students through an experience that gets everyone talking about teaching and learning.

Christine's Reflection

I have been fortunate to have developed an SGID program in collaboration with a great team within our center at Grand Valley State University. Every step of the way, from the design of our SGID request form to training new consultants, rich discussions have ensued. Although the decision points and potential applications that we have described in this book are many in number, for me, all of these aspects of an SGID program have provided rich opportunities to reflect deeply on the work of our center. The research that we carried out in the process of writing this book has shown that we are not alone in having enthusiastically embraced the SGID as a truly transformative practice.

In the course of my educational development work, I often remind others that teaching is a lifelong endeavor, replete with continual learning and change. This richness of experience is part of what fuels me as both an educator and educational developer. The SGID holds a similar place in my work. Over the past 10 years, our center team has made changes to the SGID program to streamline the "user experience" for instructors, enrich our collective instructional consultant skills, and meaningfully integrate the SGID into center initiatives. Despite this continuous improvement, the SGID remains a steadfast component of our center's portfolio and I do not expect that to change anytime soon.

I would be remiss if I didn't reflect upon how each and every semester, with each SGID, I am reminded of the incredible privilege it is to learn from instructors and students. Every SGID informs my own thinking about the enterprise of teaching and learning, the practice of educational development, and my own approaches to teaching. It never gets old. I continue to stand in awe of the ways in which the SGID not only fulfills the promise of a midsemester correction but also so deeply impacts everyone involved: the instructor, the consultant, and the students.

Sample SGID Reports

Option 1: Grand Valley State University

This is a confidential document intended for instructor's use only.

Date:
Faculty Consultant Name and Title:
Instructor Name:
Course Number and Name:
Course Location:

General Observations

Note. *All of the text included in the following three sections is taken directly from the students. Bracketed text is authored by the faculty consultant and is included for context and/or clarity. The * indicates a comment made by more than one group of students.*

- What HELPS your learning?
- What HINDERS your learning?
- What SUGGESTIONS do you have to ENHANCE learning?

Option 2: Colby College

The *most* important part of the SGID is talking to your students about the results. Be prepared to comment on the results during the next class.

Instructor:
Course:
Consultant:
Date:
Themes: (2–3 themes that reflect the conversation with the students about their feedback)

Student Feedback

- What are you doing that helps your learning in this course?
- What are you doing that hinders your learning in this course? What could you do to improve your learning in this course?
- What helps your learning in this course?
- What hinders your learning in this course?
- What suggestions do you have to improve your learning in this class?

APPENDIX B

SGID Consultant Manual

*Grand Valley State University, Pew Faculty Teaching and
Learning Center*

Manual Contents

    I. Program Overview
    II. Communications
    III. Classroom Instructions
    IV. Report Preparation and Instructor Meeting

I. Mid-Semester Interview About Teaching (MIT) Program Overview

What Is a "MIT"?

The MIT is a midsemester evaluation technique that provides instructors useful, formative feedback from their students about their learning in a course. The service involves a faculty consultant from the Pew FTLC visiting your classroom, interviewing your students, and reporting the feedback to you in a private follow-up consultation.

How Much Time Is Involved in the Process?

The faculty consultant will use approximately 30–40 minutes of class time to conduct the interview. Your follow-up meeting with the faculty consultant will typically take anywhere between 20 and 60 minutes, depending on the nature of the material, the size of the class, and the desire of the instructor. We recommend that you reserve 10–15 minutes to review the student feedback with your students at the class directly following the MIT.

Why Should I Gather Feedback Midsemester?

Course evaluations given at the end of the semester, although useful in their own right, do not help faculty members while the course is still in progress.

The purposes of gathering informal feedback from your students at midsemester are to

1. allow you to gather formative feedback that is separate from the summative student evaluations used in the personnel process;
2. allow you to correct student misconceptions, alleviate concerns, or to make changes to the course schedule, activities, and so on, before the end of the semester if necessary;
3. communicate to students that you care about their input; and
4. provide an opportunity for students to reflect on their own expectations, efforts, and learning.

The additional benefits of inviting a Pew FTLC consultant to conduct a midsemester interview are to

1. allow students to express feedback with anonymity;
2. allow a neutral party to interface with students to seek clarification and consensus; and
3. offer the instructor a resource with whom they may consult, brainstorm, and/or problem-solve in response to the student feedback.

The MIT is a completely confidential process conducted by a neutral party. It is conducted in service to you and your students, and is in no way intended to be a part of the summative personnel process.

How Does the Process Work?

The MIT involves a Pew FTLC faculty consultant visiting your class between the 4th and 9th week of the semester. He/she will meet with your students (in your absence) for either the first or last 30–40 minutes of class. During this time, the consultant will ask your students three questions:

- What *helps* your learning in this course?
- What *hinders* your learning in this course?
- What suggestions do you have to enhance your learning in this course?

Students will be separated into small groups in which they will briefly discuss their response to these questions and report their responses on the whiteboard. The consultant will facilitate a class discussion, seeking clarification and consensus. At the end of the interview, the consultant will capture the responses from the whiteboard and transcribe the data into a confidential written document which will be shared with only you in a confidential follow-up consultation meeting. The follow-up meeting may also be used to address questions, share ideas, and problem-solve as needed. When possible, follow-up meetings will be scheduled promptly after the classroom interview and before the next class meeting.

How Do I Respond to the Feedback?

Promptly responding to the feedback is a critical step in the process. Directly after your follow-up consultation meeting, take some time to absorb the positive comments students made. Keep in mind that it isn't always easy to receive feedback. Focusing on the positive comments first will likely help you to better accept the suggestions for improvement. Identify the suggestions for improvement in three categories:

> Those that can be implemented immediately this semester
> Those that will have to wait until the next time the course is offered
> Those that are simply unrealistic.

At the first class after the interview, begin by letting the students know that you heard their suggestions and appreciate the feedback. Reporting back to the students can take the form of a discussion, handout, PowerPoint presentation, or summary document posted on Blackboard. The most important thing is to let students know that you take their feedback seriously. If you decide to change something about the course as a result of student feedback, let the students know. If there are suggestions that have to wait until the next course offering, let the students know why. Acknowledging the third category of feedback during class gives you a chance to remind students of the pedagogical value of certain course elements that they might wish would go away (exams, finals, projects, etc.). As the semester progresses, remind students of any changes that you have made.

II. MIT Consultant Communications

Email to Instructor (Before MIT)

- Confirm the date, time, and location of the MIT. (*Note.* The last 30 minutes of class is preferable, but particularly for night classes, the first 30 minutes of class is also an option.)
- Request an electronic copy of the course syllabus.

Meeting (or Phone Call) With Instructor (Before MIT)

- Review the process, answer any questions, and remind instructor of the following details:
  - ○ Do not tell students about the event in advance.
  - ○ Consultant will arrive 5–10 minutes early to sit in with class.
  - ○ Remember to introduce consultant to the class.
  - ○ Do not remain anywhere near the classroom during the MIT.
  - ○ Follow up with your students at the next class.
- Inquire about any special concerns or areas of focus for the interview.
- Confirm number of students enrolled in the course (record on MIT Worksheet).
- Confirm the presence of a whiteboard in the classroom.
- Get an emergency contact number.
- Set up a post-MIT meeting time. (*Note.* It is best to meet the following day, but any time before the next class will work.)

Email to Instructor (after MIT)

- Thank the instructor for inviting you to the class.
- Confirm your post-MIT meeting time and location.

Email to Instructor (After MIT Debrief)

- Congratulate instructor on participating in the process.
- Reiterate some of the positive aspects of the MIT feedback.
- Provide additional links to resources that you may have discussed with the instructor.
- Remind the instructor of other FTLC offerings that may be of interest to them.

III. MIT Classroom Instructions

Bring:

- MIT KIT (dry erase markers, whiteboard cleaner, writing utensil, notepad, MIT classroom instructions)
- GVSU name tag
- Course syllabus (for reference)
- Additional notes from instructor (if applicable)
- Phone/camera to capture the whiteboard
- Poster paper/flip chart (if no whiteboard is available)

Arrival (5–10 Minutes)

- Arrive about 5–10 minutes early and quietly sit in the back of the classroom to observe the class. This signals the instructor to wrap up their work in preparation for the MIT.
- While casually observing the class, you may want to take some notes to include in the MIT report about the dynamic/energy of the classroom and the approximate number of students present.

Introduction (2–3 Minutes)

- Introduce yourself as a faculty member and consultant for the Pew FTLC.
- Thank the instructor for the invitation to his/her classroom and wait for him/her to leave the room. Be sure to close the classroom door before proceeding.
- Write your name and email on the board for the students' reference.
- Describe the MIT process as follows.

Role of Instructor

- The MIT is a VOLUNTARY process initiated by the instructor to gather midsemester student feedback on the learning environment in the current course. This tool is formative and confidential and in no way connected to a summative evaluation of your instructor.
- Instructors typically request a MIT because they care about the quality of your learning experience and want to invite an active dialogue around what may or may not enhance your learning going forward.
- Although a MIT does not guarantee a change to the course, it does provide an opportunity for students to reflect on their learning and share their feedback with the instructor anonymously.

Role of MIT Consultant

- As the facilitator, I will conduct the interview, maintain your individual anonymity, collect and deliver your feedback to your instructor accurately and completely, and meet with your instructor as a follow-up.

Role of Students

- This process is about improving the learning in the class, not necessarily about making it easier. Suggestions should be actionable items that contribute to learning.

- Do not assume that your instructor already knows what he/she does well.
- Constructive criticism about your learning is not disrespectful to your instructor.
- Clear and specific feedback is more likely to positively influence instructor response.
- Not all issues can or will be resolved during the course of this semester, but they will be included in the dialogue.

Discussion (5–7 Minutes)

- Invite the students to work in small groups of 4–6 people (bigger groups for bigger classes to make best use of the time) to answer the following questions:
  - What *helps* your learning in this course?
  - What *hinders* your learning in this course?
  - What *suggestions* do you have to improve your learning in this course?
- While students are discussing, write the questions on the board, keeping in mind that you will need to easily capture the data with a camera.
- Invite one person from each group to record responses on the board. Encourage students to asterisk a response if they share the opinion of another group in order to avoid redundant comments.
- Continue to circulate through the room listening and observing.
- As students move to the board to record their feedback, engage the remaining students in general questions about their demographic (year in school, major, required course, first course with this professor, etc.). This context may become useful in better understanding the feedback. It also keeps the students engaged in the process.

Interview (15–20 Minutes)

- Ask questions to clarify and to provide examples of the feedback given.
- Stay neutral. Avoid leading or accusatory questions. Resist the urge to interpret or defend either the instructor or the students.
- Ask students to raise their hand to comment and cease all private conversations.
- Repeat the comments to be sure you understand.
- Make note when students seem divided on an issue.
- Do not discuss everything on the board. Try to link common threads.
- Begin with the "Help" category to set a positive tone.

- Pair "Hinder" category with "Suggestion" category. Don't leave a hindrance as a complaint with no suggestion.
- Ask about the instructor's specific concerns when applicable.

Wrap-Up (2–3 Minutes)

- Thank the class for their participation.
- Notify students that you will be meeting with their instructor to deliver the feedback and that their instructor will discuss the feedback with them at their next class meeting.
- Take a picture of the board.
- Close the door after students leave to protect the anonymity of the data on the board.
- Do not forget to thoroughly erase the board!

IV. Report Preparation and Instructor Meeting

Prepare MIT Report

- List the instructor name, course name & number, date and time of class, and name of consultant.
- Capture the student comments "as is" from the board and include them in three separate sections ("Helps," "Hinders," "Suggestions").
- If you choose to add notes about your own impression of the classroom or add clarifying comments to those of the students, be sure to distinguish them from the student's comments (i.e. use brackets).

Instructor Meeting

- Remind instructor that the process is confidential.
- Review the feedback with the instructor. (Note: Do not give them the written feedback until you are finished reviewing as they can distract the instructor from the conversation.)
- Rally behind the instructor.
- Share ideas, articles, and/or effective teaching strategies.
- Suggest small mid-course corrections that can easily be implemented this semester.
- Remind the instructor to discuss the feedback at the next class.
- Destroy the electronic copy of the feedback.

APPENDIX C

SGID Marketing Emails and Registration Form

Marketing Message—Colby College

If you are interested in collecting midsemester course feedback from your students, consider requesting a Mid-Semester Course Analysis (MSCA). During this learner-centered process, a faculty consultant from the Center for Teaching and Learning will visit your class for 30 minutes and work with your students to discuss things that are helping and hindering their learning. The process involves asking your students to reflect on how the course (your instruction) and their participation impact learning. You are not present for this conversation. The consultant will meet with you after the session to discuss the implications of the results.

The Center for Teaching and Learning will be offering MSCAs from Monday 9/30 until Friday 11/1, except during Fall Break (10/21 and 10/22). Click on the following link to submit your request by Monday, September 16. The CTL has a limited capacity but hopes to accommodate all requests. *MSCA registration link.*

Marketing Message (Sample 1)—Grand Valley State University

The MIT is a midsemester evaluation technique that provides instructors useful feedback from their students about their learning in a course. The service involves a faculty consultant from the Pew Faculty Teaching and Learning Center visiting the instructor's class, interviewing students, and reporting back to the instructor in a private follow-up consultation. Conducted during the 4th to 9th week of the semester, the MIT takes 30–40 minutes of class time. The instructor will need to schedule an additional 10–15 minutes during the class directly following the MIT to review the feedback with students.

> MIT Period, Fall 2014: September 15—October 24
> Please visit www.gvsu.edu/ftlc/mitinfo for additional details and a
>   link to an online request form.
> Suggested Request Deadline, Fall 2014: Monday, September 29

Marketing Message (Sample 2)—Grand Valley State University

We would like to remind you of the innovative evaluative mechanism that the Pew Faculty Teaching and Learning Center offers each semester—the Mid-Semester Interview About Teaching (MIT). The MIT is a midsemester evaluation technique that provides instructors useful and timely feedback from their students about their learning in a course. The process is voluntary, confidential, and not part of the of GVSU personnel policy. Research (Diamond, 2004) has shown that it is a "useful tool in motivating, creating, and maintaining change among faculty in efforts to strengthen their teaching" (p. 227).

The process involves a faculty consultant from the Pew FTLC visiting your class, interviewing students, and reporting back to you in a private follow-up consultation. Conducted during the 4th to 9th week of the semester, the MIT takes 30–40 minutes of class time. An additional 10–15 minutes of class time is needed to review the student feedback with your students during the class directly following the MIT.

Please visit www.gvsu.edu/ftlc/mitinfo for additional details and a link to an online request form.

Sample SGID Registration Items

Demographic Information

- First Name, Last Name (use separate fields to allow sorting by last name)
- Email address
- Pronouns
- Department or Program

Course Details

- Course Number
- Course Name
- Number of Students
- Classroom Location
- Class Start Time
- Class End Time

SGID Details

- SGID Date—1st Choice
- SGID Date—2nd Choice

Connecting Consultant to Instructor

Sample Email 1 (Colby College—from the CTL to Instructor; Consultant CC'd on Email)

Dear (Instructor First Name),

The consultant for the Mid-Semester Course Analysis (MSCA) you requested for your (Course Number)—(Course Name) course is (Consultant Name), cc'd on this message. The consultant will arrive to your class in (Classroom Location) on (MSCA Date) at (Arrival Time), to start the consultation with your students at (Start Time). Typically, the MSCA process takes about 30 minutes, where the students work in small groups to answer a few questions about the course and about their participation in the course. Then they put their feedback up on the board and spend about 15 minutes talking about their responses with the consultant.

Tips to Ensure a Successful MSCA

- You don't need to tell your students this is going to happen in class—that way they enter the process with a fresh perspective.
- You don't need to explain the process to them when the consultant arrives—they will do that after you leave.
- You do need to set up a meeting within a few days after the MSCA with your consultant to discuss the results. *Please send your consultant a few times for the day of or after your MSCA that you are free to meet with the consultant.*
- You do need to follow up with your students after your conversation with the consultant.

What Your Consultant Needs From You

- A copy of your syllabus
- Knowledge of your classroom—what kind of writing surface is there (whiteboard, blackboard)?
- Any concerns you might have about the course that the consultant should be aware of. We like to have a fresh perspective on the feedback, but sometimes it can be helpful to know your concerns.

Sincerely, (Name of MSCA Coordinator)

Sample Email 2 (Grand Valley State University—From the Consultant to the Instructor Directly)

Dear (Instructor Name),

Thank you for requesting a Mid-Semester Interview about Teaching (MIT). I am looking forward to working with you. The purpose of this email is to confirm the specific time and location of my visit to your classroom on (date). The interview will take approximately 30 minutes. It is preferable to conduct the MIT during the last 30 minutes of class, but I am willing to accommodate what is best for your particular circumstance. Please let me know. Also I would like to request the following information in preparation for my visit: (a) your availability on (date) for a follow-up meeting in my office, (b) an electronic copy of the course syllabus, (c) an emergency contact number in the event of a last-minute delay or cancellation, (d) the presence of a whiteboard in your classroom, and (e) any special concerns or areas of focus you would like me to address in the interview.

Sincerely, (Consultant Name)

SGID Follow-Up Email Contents

After Classroom Session With Students

- Thank the instructor for inviting you to the class.
- Confirm post-SGID meeting time and location.

After Consultation With Instructor

- Congratulate instructor on participating in the process.
- Reiterate some of the positive aspects of the SGID feedback.
- Provide additional links to resources that you may have discussed with the instructor.
- Remind the instructor of other programs that may be of interest to them.

SGID Case Studies

Cara Meixner and Carol A. Hurney (used with permission)

The cases were designed to give consultants training dealing with different kinds of instructors—apathetic instructors (Annabella), instructors with habits the students found distracting (Paul), instructors with challenging personalities (Ricki), and instructors who are nervous about what the students might say about them (Norm). These cases include the SGID results from the student session along with a bit of backstory. A few of the cases include the learner-centered SGID questions, which ask students to reflect on their role in the learning process. Depending upon the needs of the consultants, training sessions with these cases could involve the development of summaries or themes from the student feedback, development of strategies to approach the conversation with the instructor, and/or role-playing experiences that allow consultants to refine ways they approach different instructors and different kinds of SGID results.

Annabella

Imagine that you are the SGID consultant for Annabella's introductory, required course of 79 students (results follow). As you discuss hindrances and suggestions with the faculty member, she casually interrupts and says, "You don't really think I'm going to change anything, do you? I mean, these are just a bunch of silly gripes that don't merit my attention."

What Helps Your Learning?

- Examples
- Online quizzes
- Real-world examples
- Going over tests in class
- Accessible for questions
- Keeps us engaged

- Helpful during office hours
- Humor
- Homework
- Working out problems on the board
- Test materials taught in class

What Hinders Your Learning

- Errors in the text
- Not clarifying what we should know for tests, and so on.
- Questions from students lead to unnecessary topics
- Not fully explaining lingo
- Too much data on the PowerPoint slides
- Fast-paced
- Answers are too similar on tests—questions should be less debatable

What Suggestions Do You Have to Improve Your Learning in This Class?

- Extra credit
- Quicker replies to email
- Suggest specific book problems to work on
- Work more book problems in class
- Only answer intelligent questions, not silly ones

Paul

Imagine that you are the SGID consultant and what follows are the results from one of your first SGIDs of the semester. The students note how distracted they get by the professor's incessant pacing in front of the lectern. The class isn't entirely delivered in lecture format, but when it is, the students tune out.

What Helps Your Learning in This Course?

- Group activities
- Video clips
- PowerPoints
- Personal, practical examples
- Interactive teaching
- Faculty is easygoing and energetic

What Hinders Your Learning in This Course?

- Keeps pacing in front of lectern
- Lecture without activities
- Readings—sometimes they complement the class, sometimes they don't

What Suggestions Do You Have to Improve Your Learning in This Course?

- Make reviews more frequent
- Study guides

What Are You Doing to Help Your Learning in This Course?

- Going to class
- Studying the visual aids/PowerPoints
- Being serious about group activities
- Participating in class and listening
- Reading the material

What Are You Doing to Hinder Your Learning in This Course?

- Getting distracted by our work for other classes
- Not studying long enough
- Sleeping or daydreaming
- Not reading book

What Could You Be Doing to Improve Your Learning in This Course?

- Read more carefully
- Study longer
- Go to office hours

Ricki

Imagine that you are the SGID consultant for Ricki's 300-level course. During the SGID, two student groups remark that they perceive the professor to be arrogant (SGID results follow). Based on your impressions of Ricki, this feedback surprises you. From your perspective, Ricki seems confident, intelligent, and opinionated—but not arrogant. When you provide them students' feedback during the consultation meeting—and the context they provided—they admit to being shocked. "Nothing else comes as a surprise," they say, "but I just can't believe they see me as arrogant. That's just not who I am." Then, they ask, "How do I respond to feedback like that? I mean, what could I say or do when, clearly, the students' minds are probably already made up about me."

What Helps Your Learning in This Course?

- PowerPoints
- YouTube videos
- Current events
- Real-world examples
- Personal experience stories
- Encouraging office hours

What Hinders Your Learning in This Course?

- Not having PowerPoints posted
- Too many out-of-class assignments—hard to keep up
- Bad communication on assignments
- Professor seems arrogant
- In-class quizzes
- Informational interviews—too much else to do

What Suggestions Do You Have to Improve Your Learning in This Course?

- Post PowerPoint slides
- Better communication—legitimate calendar
- Make quizzes take-home
- More broad concepts on quizzes that relate to the class
- Fewer short-answer questions on tests

What Are You Doing to Help Your Learning in This Course?

- Taking notes
- Reading outside texts
- Paying attention
- Coming to class

What Are You Doing to Hinder Your Learning in This Course?

- Procrastination
- Not initially taking notes because expected notes online
- Taking other courses

What Could You Be Doing to Improve Your Learning in This Course?

- Go to office hours
- Group study sessions
- Not procrastinate

Norm

Imagine that you are the SGID consultant for this introductory computer science class. The SGID conversation with the students went well, but when you initially talked to the faculty member on the telephone before the SGID, he seemed very nervous. When you appeared in class, he said under his tongue, "I hope they don't skewer me or I'll probably lose my job." You've just begun the SGID consultation and notice that he's more anxious than ever.

What Helps Your Learning?

- Instructor is enthusiastic, personable, approachable
- Hands-on activities (although being in a computer lab might overemphasize computer applications)
- Relating to practical placements
- Group work
- Outside observation
- Discussing assignments in detail

What Hinders Your Learning?

- Excessive expectations for 3-credit class
- Grades do not reflect amount of effort done outside of class
- Concepts not well structured, nor organized in sequence
- Assignments too numerous, lengthy, not well related to real-world experiences
- Expectations unclear; feedback delayed and vague
- Previous course not good foundation, but other courses could be drawn upon

What Suggestions Do You Have to Improve Your Learning in This Class?

- Structure concepts ("topic of the day") and transitions
- Share more of own experiences, specific examples
- Simplify assignments, clarify expectations

- Provide examples of more nonsoftware approaches
- Provide success criteria so more likely can earn full credit on assignments
- More practical examples

REFERENCES

Abbott, R. D., Wulff, D. H., Nyquist, J. D., Ropp, V. A., & Hess, C. W. (1990). Satisfaction with processes of collecting student opinions about instruction: The student perspective. *Journal of Educational Psychology, 82*(2), 201–206. https://doi.org/10.1037/0022-0663.82.2.201

Ackerman, D. S., Gross, B. L., & Vigneron, F. (2009). Peer observation reports and student evaluations of teaching: Who are the experts? *The Alberta Journal of Educational Research, 55*(1), 18–39.

Ambady, N., & Rosenthal, R. (1993). Half a minute: Predicting teacher evaluations from thin slices of nonverbal behavior and physical attractiveness. *Journal of Personality and Social Psychology, 64*(3), 431–441. https://doi.org/10.1037/0022-3514.64.3.431

Angelo, T. A., & Cross, K. P. (1993). *Classroom assessment techniques: A handbook for college teachers* (2nd ed.). Jossey-Bass.

Bartholomew, T., Wright, M. C., & Michaels, C. (2018). Partnering with teaching and learning centers for curricular assessment: A case study of best practices. In C. J. Stanny (Ed.), *Assessment in action: Evidence-based discussions about teaching, learning, and curriculum* (New Directions for Teaching and Learning, no. 155, pp. 21–29). Jossey-Bass. https://doi.org/10.1002/tl.20299

Bazeley, J., Haynes, C., Myers, C. S., & Resnis, E. (2019). Avoiding the "axe": Advancing affordable and open education resources at a midsize university. *Journal of Librarianship and Scholarly Communication, 7* (General Issue). https://doi.org/10.7710/2162-3309.2259

Beach, A. L., Sorcinelli, M. D., Austin, A. E., & Rivard, J. K. (2016). *Faculty development in the age of evidence: Current practices, future imperatives.* Stylus.

Black, B. (1998). Using the SGID method for a variety of purposes. *To Improve the Academy, 17*, 245–262. https://doi.org/10.1002/j.2334-4822.1998.tb00352.x

Blash, A., Schneller, B., Hunt, J., Michaels, N., & Thorndike, J. (2018). There's got to be a better way! Introducing faculty to mid-course formative reviews as a constructive tool for growth and development. *Currents in Pharmacy Teaching and Learning, 10*(9), 1228–1236. https://doi.org/10.1016/j.cptl.2018.06.015

Blue, J., Wentzell, G. W., & Evins, M. J. (2014). What do students want? Small group instructional diagnoses of STEM faculty. In P. V. Engelhardt, A. D. Churukian, & D. L. Jones (Eds.), *2014 PERC Proceedings* (pp. 43–46). American Association of Physics Teachers. https://doi.org/10.1119/perc.2014.pr.007

Blumberg, P. (2019). *Making learning-centered teaching work: Practical strategies for implementation.* Stylus.

Bowden, D. (2004). Small group instructional diagnosis: A method for enhancing writing instruction. *WPA: Writing Program Administration, 28*(1–2), 115–135. http://associationdatabase.co/archives/28n1-2/28n1-2bowden.pdf

Boysen, G. A., Richmond, A. S., & Gurung, R. A. R. (2015). Model teaching criteria for psychology: Initial documentation of teacher's self-reported competency. *Scholarship of Teaching and Learning in Psychology, 1*(1), 48–59. https://doi.org/10.1037/stl0000023

Brinko, K. T. (1997). The interactions of teaching improvement. In K. T. Brinko & R. J. Menges (Eds.), *Practically speaking: A sourcebook for instructional consultants in higher education* (pp. 3–8). New Forums Press.

Brown, M. J. (2008). Student perceptions of teaching evaluations. *Journal of Instructional Psychology, 35*(2), 177–181. https://doi.org/10.1177/0098628315603062

Chávez, A. F., & Longerbeam, S. D. (2016). *Teaching across cultural strengths: A guide to balancing integrated and individuated cultural frameworks in college teaching.* Stylus.

Chen, B., Van Assche, J., Vansteenkiste, M., Soenens, B., & Beyers, W. (2015). Does psychological need satisfaction matter when environmental or financial safety are at risk? *Journal of Happiness Studies, 16*(3), 745–766. https://doi.org/10.1007/s10902-014-9532-5

Clark, D. J., & Redmond, M. V. (1982). *Small group instructional diagnosis: Final report* [ED217954]. ERIC. https://files.eric.ed.gov/fulltext/ED217954.pdf

Coffman, S. J. (1998). Small group instructional evaluation across disciplines. *College Teaching, 46*(3), 106–111. https://doi.org/10.1080/87567559809596250

Cohen, P. A. (1980). Effectiveness of student-rating feedback for improving college instruction: A meta-analysis of findings. *Research in Higher Education, 13*(4), 321–341. https://doi.org/10.1007/BF00976252

Cook-Sather, A. (2009). From traditional accountability to shared responsibility: The benefits and challenges of student consultants gathering midcourse feedback in college classrooms. *Assessment & Evaluation in Higher Education, 34*(2), 231–241. https://doi.org/10.1080/02602930801956042

Cook-Sather, A., Bovill, C., & Felten, P. (2014). *Engaging students as partners in learning and teaching: A guide for faculty.* Jossey-Bass.

Cox, M. D., & Sorenson, D. L. (2000). Student collaboration in faculty development: Connecting directly to the learning revolution. *To Improve the Academy, 18*(1), 97–127. https://doi.org/10.1002/j.2334-4822.2000.tb00365.x

Craig, M. (2007). Facilitated student discussions for evaluating teaching. *ACM SIGCSE Bulletin, 39*(1), 190–194. https://doi.org/10.1145/1227310.1227376

Crow, R., McGinty, D., & LeBaron, J. (2008). The Online Small Group Analysis (OSGA): Adapting a tested formative assessment technique for online teaching. *MountainRise, 4*(3), 1–18.

Crowne, D. P., & Marlowe, D. (1960). A new scale of social desirability independent of psychopathology. *Journal of Consulting Psychology, 24*(4), 349–354. https://doi.org/10.1037/h0047358

Deci, E. L., & Ryan, R. M. (2000). The "what" and "why" of goal pursuits: Human needs and the self-determination of behavior. *Psychological Inquiry, 11*(4), 227–268. https://doi.org/10.1207/S15327965PLI1104_01

Diamond, M. R. (2004). The usefulness of structured mid-term feedback as a catalyst for change in higher education classes. *Active Learning in Higher Education, 5*(3), 217–231. https://doi.org/10.1177/1469787404046845

Finelli, C. J., Ott, M., Gottfried, A. C., Hershock, C., O'Neal, C., & Kaplan, M. (2008). Utilizing instructional consultations to enhance the teaching performance of engineering faculty. *Journal of Engineering Education, 97*(4), 397–411. https://doi.org/10.1002/j.2168-9830.2008.tb00989.x

Finelli, C. J., Pinder-Grover, T., & Wright, M. C. (2011). Consultations on teaching. Using student feedback for instructional improvement. In C. E. Cook & M. L. Kaplan (Eds.), *Advancing the culture of teaching at a research university: How a teaching center can make a difference* (pp. 65–79). Stylus.

Fink, L. D., & Sorenson, D. L. (2012). Developing professional expertise. In K. T. Brinko & R. J. Mendes (Eds.), *Practically speaking: A sourcebook for instructional consultants in higher education* (pp. 147–152). New Forums Press.

Gollwitzer, P. M. (1999). Implementation intentions: Strong effects of simple plans. *American Psychologist, 54*(7), 493–503. https://doi.org/10.1037/0003-066X.54.7.493

Gooder, V., & Cantwell, S. (2017). Student experiences with a newly developed concept-based curriculum. *Teaching and Learning in Nursing, 12*(2), 142–147. https://doi.org/10.1016/j.teln.2016.11.002

Harper, L. M., Maden, M., & Dickson, R. (2020). Across five levels: The evidence of impact model. *Evaluation, 26*(3), 350–366. https://doi.org/10.1177/1356389019850844

Heppner, P. P., & Johnston, J. A. (1994). Peer consultation: Faculty and students working together to improve teaching. *Journal of Counseling & Development, 72*(5), 492–499. https://doi.org/10.1002/j.1556-6676.1994.tb00979.x

Holton, D., Mahmood, H., Cunningham, K., Diamond, M. R., Wright, M., Bali, M., Brown, S., & Domínguez, E. (2016). *Midterm student feedback guidebook.* http://bit.ly/msfguidebook

Hunt, N. (2003). Does mid-semester feedback make a difference? *The Journal of Scholarship of Teaching and Learning, 3*(2), 13–20.

Hurney, C. A., Harris, N. L., Bates Prins, S. C., & Kruck, S. E. (2014). The impact of a learner-centered, mid-semester course evaluation on students. *Journal of Faculty Development, 28*(3), 55–62.

Hurney, C. A., Troisi, J. D., & Leaman, L. H. (2020). Development of a faculty appreciation of pedagogy scale. *To Improve the Academy, 39*(2), 27–50. https://doi.org/10.3998/tia.17063888.0039.202

Hutchinson, A., & Stoeckle, A. (2020). Using mid-semester assessment programs (MAPs) as a catalyst for the scholarship of teaching and learning (SoTL). In R. C. Plews & M. L. Amos (Eds.), *Evidence-based faculty development through the scholarship of teaching and learning* (pp. 181–200). IGI Global. https://doi.org/10.4018/978-1-7998-2212-7.ch010

Katz, J., & Henry, M. (1988). *Turning professors into teachers: A new approach to faculty development and student learning.* Macmillan.

Keeley, J. W., Furr, R. M., & Buskist, W. (2010). Differentiating psychology students' perceptions of teachers using the Teacher Behavior Checklist. *Teaching of Psychology, 37*(1), 16–20. https://doi.org/10.1080/00986280903426282

Keeley, J. W., Ismail, E., & Buskist, W. (2016). Excellent teachers' perspectives on excellent teaching. *Teaching of Psychology, 43*(3), 175–179. https://doi.org/10.1177/0098628316649307

Keeley, J. W., Smith, D., & Buskist, W. (2006). The Teacher Behaviors Checklist: Factor analysis of its utility for evaluating teaching. *Teaching of Psychology, 33*(2), 84–91. https://doi.org/10.1207/s15328023top3302_1

Kiesler, C. A. (1971). *Psychology of commitment: Experiments linking behavior to belief.* Academic Press.

Kolb, D. A. (2015). *Experiential learning: Experience as the source of learning and development* (2nd ed.). Pearson.

Lammers, W. J., Gillaspy, J. A., Jr., & Hancock, F. (2017). Predicting academic success with early, middle, and late semester assessment of student-instructor rapport. *Teaching of Psychology, 44*(2), 145–149. https://doi.org/10.1177/0098628317692618

Lang, J. M. (2016). *Small teaching: Everyday lessons from the science of learning.* John Wiley & Sons.

Legg, A. M., & Wilson, J. H. (2009). E-mail from professor enhances student motivation and attitudes. *Teaching of Psychology, 36*(3), 205–211. https://doi.org/10.1080/00986280902960034

Lerner, J. S., & Tetlock, P. E. (1999). Accounting for the effects of accountability. *Psychological Bulletin, 125*(2), 255–275. https://doi.org/10.1037/0033-2909.125.2.255

Lewis, K. G. (2001). Using midsemester student feedback and responding to it. In K. G. Lewis (Ed.), *Techniques and strategies for interpreting student evaluations* (New Directions for Teaching and Learning, no. 87, pp. 33–44). Jossey-Bass.

Little, D., & Palmer, M. (2012). Training instructional consultants to use a coaching framework. In K. T. Brinko (Ed.), *Practically speaking: A sourcebook for instructional consultants in higher education* (2nd ed.; pp. 208–216). Stylus.

Mauger, D. (2010). *Small group instructional feedback: A student perspective of its impact on the teaching and learning environment* (Publication No. 3407167) [Doctoral dissertation, George Fox University]. ProQuest Dissertations & Theses Global.

McDonnell, G. P., & Dodd, M. D. (2017). Should students have the power to change course structure? *Teaching of Psychology, 44*(2), 91–99. https://doi.org/10.1177/0098628317692604

McGowan, W. R. (2009). *Faculty and student perceptions of the effects of mid-course evaluations on learning and teaching* (Publication No. 3376925) [Doctoral dissertation, Brigham Young University]. ProQuest Dissertations & Theses Global.

Millis, B. J., & Vazquez, J. (2010). Down with SGID! Long live QCD! *Essays on Teaching Excellence: Toward the Best in the Academy, 22*(4), 1–5. https://podnetwork.org/content/uploads/V22_N4_Millis_Vasquez.pdf

Newby, T., Sherman, M., & Coffman, S. J. (1991, April 1). *Instructional diagnosis: Effective open-ended faculty evaluation* [Conference session]. The Annual Meeting of the American Educational Research Association, Chicago, IL, United States.

O'Neal-Hixon, K., Long, J., & Bock, M. (2017). The eSGID Process: How to improve teaching and learning in online graduate courses. *The Journal of Effective Teaching, 17*(2), 45–57. https://files.eric.ed.gov/fulltext/EJ1157448.pdf

Overall, J. U., & Marsh, H. W. (1979). Midterm feedback from students: Its relationship to instructional improvement and students' cognitive and affective outcomes. *Journal of Educational Psychology, 71*(6), 856. https://doi.org/10.1037/0022-0663.71.6.856

Payette, P. R., & Brown, M. K. (2018, January). *Gathering mid-semester feedback: Three variations to improve instruction.* https://ideacontent.blob.core.windows.net/content/sites/2/2020/01/PaperIDEA_67.pdf

Penny, A. R., & Coe, R. (2004). Effectiveness of consultation on student ratings feedback: A meta-analysis. *Review of Educational Research, 74*(2), 215–253. https://doi.org/10.3102/00346543074002215

Piccinin, S. (1999). How individual consultation affects teaching. In C. G. Knapper & S. Piccinin (Eds.), *Taking small group learning online: Best practices for team-based learning* (New Directions for Teaching and Learning, no. 70, pp. 71–83). Jossey-Bass.

Pink, D. H. (2018). *When: The scientific secrets of perfect timing.* Riverhead Books.

Redmond, M. V. (1982). *A process of midterm evaluation incorporating small group discussion of a course and its effects on student motivation* (ED217953). https://files.eric.ed.gov/fulltext/ED217953.pdf

Remington, T. L., Hershock, C., Klein, K., Niemer, R. K., & Bleske, B. E. (2015). Lessons from the trenches: Implementing team-based learning across several courses. *Currents in Pharmacy Teaching and Learning, 7*, 121–130. https://doi.org/10.1016/j.cptl.2014.09.008

Richmond, A. S., Boysen, G. A., & Gurung, R. A. R. (2016). *An evidence-based guide to college and university teaching: Developing the model teacher.* Routledge.

Robinson, K. (1995). *Using small group instructional feedback (SGIF) as an alternative to mid-course questionnaires: Practical guidelines for instructors and facilitators* (ED420346). ERIC. https://files.eric.ed.gov/fulltext/ED420346.pdf

Ryan, R. G., Wilson, J. H., & Pugh, J. L. (2011). Psychometric characteristics of the professor-student rapport scale. *Teaching of Psychology, 38*(3), 135–141. https://doi.org/10.1177/0098628311411894

Ryan, R. M., & Deci, E. L. (2000). Self-determination theory and the facilitation of intrinsic motivation, social development, and well-being. *American Psychologist, 55*(1), 68–78. https://doi.org/10.1037/0003-066X.55.1.68

Ryan, R. M., & Deci, E. L. (2017). *Self-determination theory: Basic psychological needs in motivation, development, and wellness.* Guilford Press.

Sheldon, K. M., & Gunz, A. (2009). Psychological needs as basic motives, not just experiential requirements. *Journal of Personality, 77*(5), 1467–1492. https://doi.org/10.1111/j.1467-6494.2009.00589.x

Sherry, A. C., Fulford, C. P., & Zhang, S. (1998). Assessing distance learners' satisfaction with instruction: A quantitative and a qualitative measure. *The American Journal of Distance Education, 12*(3), 4–28. https://doi.org/10.1080/08923649809527002

Sit, S. M., & Brudzinski, M. R. (2017). Creation and assessment of an active e-learning introductory geology course. *Journal of Science Education and Technology, 26,* 629–645. https://doi.org/10.1007/s10956-017-9703-3

Snooks, M. K., Neeley, S. E., & Williamson, K. M. (2004). From SGID and GIFT to BBQ: Streamlining midterm student evaluations to improve teaching and learning. *To Improve the Academy, 22*(1), 110–124. https://doi.org/10.1002/j.2334-4822.2004.tb00405.x

Sozer, E. M., Zeybekoglu, Z., & Kaya, M. (2019). Using mid-semester course evaluation as a feedback tool for improving learning and teaching in higher education. *Assessment & Evaluation in Higher Education, 44*(7), 1003–1016. https://doi.org/10.1080/02602938.2018.1564810

Taylor, R. L., Knorr, K., Ogrodnik, M., & Sinclair, P. (2020). Seven principles for good practice in midterm student feedback. *International Journal for Academic Development, 25*(4), 350–362. https://doi.org/10.1080/1360144X.2020.1762086

Tiberius, R., Tipping, J., & Smith, R. (1997). Developmental stages of an educational consultant: Theoretical perspective. In K. T. Brinko & R. J. Menges (Eds.), *Practically speaking: A sourcebook for instructional consultants in higher education* (pp. 217–221). New Forums Press.

Troisi, J. D. (2014). Making the grade and staying engaged: The influence of student management teams on student classroom outcomes. *Teaching of Psychology, 41*(2), 99–103. https://doi.org/10.1177/0098628314530337

Troisi, J. D. (2015). Student management teams increase college students' feelings of autonomy in the classroom. *College Teaching, 63*(2), 83–89. https://doi.org/10.1080/87567555.2015.1007913

Veeck, A., O'Reilly, K., MacMillan, A., & Yu, H. (2016). The use of collaborative midterm student evaluations to provide actionable results. *Journal of Marketing Education, 38*(3), 157–169. https://doi.org/10.1177/0273475315619652

Watson, R. M., Willford, J. D., & Pfeifer, M. A. (2018). A cultured learning environment: Implementing a problem- and service-based microbiology capstone course to assess process- and skill-based learning objectives. *Interdisciplinary Journal of Problem-Based Learning, 12*(1), Article 8. https://doi.org/10.7771/1541-5015.1694

Wickramasinghe, S. R., & Timpson, W. M. (2006). Mid-semester student feedback enhances student learning. *Education for Chemical Engineers, 1*(1), 126–133. https://doi.org/10.1205/ece06012

Wilson, J. H., & Ryan, R. G. (2013). Professor-student rapport scale: Six items predict student outcomes. *Teaching of Psychology, 40*(2), 130–133. https://doi.org/10.1177/0098628312475033

Wilson-Doenges, G., & Gurung, R. A. R. (2013). Benchmarks for scholarly investigations of teaching and learning. *Australian Journal of Psychology, 65*(1), 63–70. https://doi.org/10.1111/ajpy.12011

Wilson-Doenges, G., Troisi, J. D., & Bartsch R. A. (2016). Exemplars of the gold standard in SoTL for psychology. *Scholarship of Teaching and Learning in Psychology, 2*(1), 1–12. https://doi.org/10.1037/stl0000050

Wright, M. C., Schram, L. N., & Gorman, K. S. (2015). Developmental stages of new graduate student instructional consultants: Implications for professional growth. *To Improve the Academy, 34*(1–2), 117–155. https://doi.org/10.1002/tia2.20027

Wulff, D. H., Staton-Spicer, A. Q., Hess, C. W., & Nyquist, J. D. (1985). The student perspective on evaluating teaching effectiveness. *ACA Bulletin, 53*, 39–47.

ABOUT THE AUTHORS

Carol A. Hurney earned her PhD in biology at the University of Virginia. She taught biology at James Madison University for 19 years where she also directed the faculty development center and developed an SGID program. She is currently the associate provost for faculty development and the founding director of the Center for Teaching and Learning at Colby College. Her scholarly interests include learner-centered teaching, active learning, and measuring the impact of educational development on faculty. Hurney is an active member of the New England Faculty Development Consortium (NEFDC) and the Professional and Organizational Development Network (POD), where she served on the board of both organizations and was the vice president of NEFDC (2020–2021). She currently is the president-elect of the POD Network and serves on the editorial teams of the *Journal of College Teaching* and the *Journal of General Education*. She consults with centers of teaching and learning to support strategic planning efforts and offers workshops for faculty to support their efforts to implement active learning strategies. She regularly attends and speaks at regional and national conferences on topics that span her expertise as a faculty member and educational developer.

Christine M. Rener is professor of chemistry and vice provost for instructional development and innovation at Grand Valley State University. She serves as director of the Robert and Mary Pew Faculty Teaching and Learning Center, overseeing a professional development program for over 1,700 faculty. In this role, Rener contributes to scholarly teaching initiatives across campus, bringing evidence-based practices to faculty in a wide array of disciplines. She has organized regional conferences on the scholarship of teaching and learning as well as educational development. Rener is active in several professional organizations and holds leadership positions within the Professional and Organizational Development Network in Higher Education, serving as a member of the Core Committee (board of directors) and chair of the Professional Development Committee. She has over 20 years of experience in higher education administration related to accreditation, assessment, and educational development. Rener is a frequent presenter at national and regional conferences on a range of integrative topics such as learner-centered teaching, faculty career growth, and assessment of educational development programs.

Jordan D. Troisi became the senior associate director of the Center for Teaching and Learning at Colby College in 2020, after 9 years as a professor of psychology at Widener University and The University of the South (Sewanee). He is an accomplished teacher, having earned early career awards from the Society for the Teaching of Psychology and the American Psychological Association. His work in the scholarship of teaching and learning is broad reaching, including over 25 peer-reviewed articles and chapters, which have appeared in *College Teaching, Journal of Faculty Development, Scholarship of Teaching and Learning in Psychology, Teaching of Psychology, To Improve the Academy,* and elsewhere. On the national and international stage, Troisi frequently gives invited addresses and keynotes at psychology and teaching and learning conferences (e.g., The Annual Convention for the Association for Psychological Sciences, The Annual Conference on Teaching).

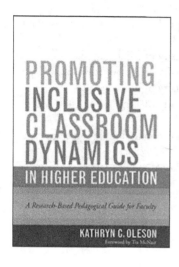

Promoting Inclusive Classroom Dynamics in Higher Education

A Research-Based Pedagogical Guide for Faculty

Kathryn C. Oleson

Foreword by Tia McNair

"Presenting research, strategies, and lived experiences in engaging and accessible ways, Kathryn C. Oleson invites us to reflect on ourselves as facilitators of learning, to recognize the necessity not just the benefits of more equitable and inclusive classrooms, and to dedicate ourselves to transforming our thinking and our practices. She provides an impressively wide range of conceptual frameworks, concrete approaches, and helpful examples that can guide the necessarily ongoing work of promoting inclusive classroom dynamics."—*Alison Cook-Sather, Professor of Education; Director of Peace, Conflict, and Social Justice Concentration; Director of Teaching and Learning Institute; Coauthor of* Promoting Equity and Justice Through Pedagogical Partnership

Taking Flight

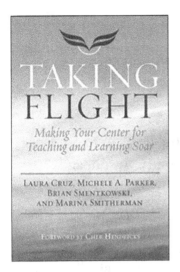

Making Your Center for Teaching and Learning Soar

Laura Cruz, Michele A. Parker, Brian Smentkowski, and Marina Smitherman

Foreword by Cher Hendricks

"*Taking Flight* is an amazing resource for everyone involved in educational development. Written in a friendly and supportive tone, the authors of this valuable resource have summarized the literature on educational development, provided examples of well-respected centers, created worksheets to help you develop your efforts, and infused their own decades of experience in this field. This book skillfully guides; it does not push. I am recommending this book to so many people."—***Todd D. Zakrajsek***, *Associate Professor, School of Medicine, University of North Carolina at Chapel Hill*